TO THE

HOOP

TO THE HOOP

Basketball and Contemporary Art

Emily Stamey
Foreword by Wes Miller

Weatherspoon Art Museum, UNC Greensboro

CONTENTS

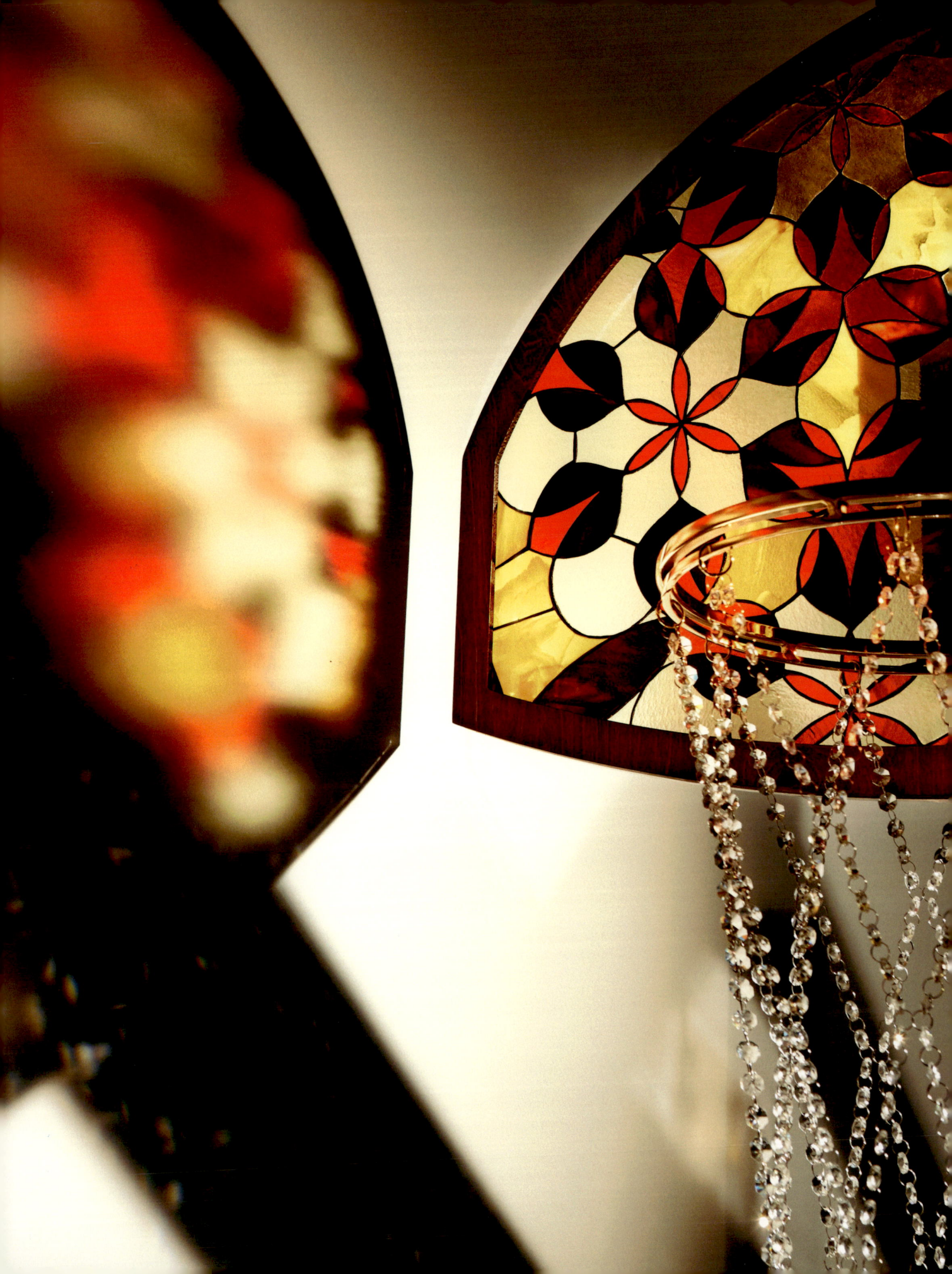

THE LOVE OF THE GAME

Wes Miller
Head Men's Basketball Coach, UNC Greensboro

Shoes squeaking, balls bouncing, the "swish" of the net when a shot hits its mark. These are the sounds of a busy workplace, the gym. When thinking of basketball in its purest form, more times than not we envision a packed arena, the crowd on its feet, that March Madness "buzz" in the air, and a game that means everything to everybody involved. What I've learned is that those images are a fantasy without the unseen hours of working in an empty gym. The squeaking shoes, the bouncing ball, the sound of a swish—those are the sounds of the off-season, an early morning in the summer, a late night in December after a tough loss.

The sweat, the burn, the energy it takes to compete and to win games—everybody wants to play on the biggest stage, but so few actually get that opportunity. All but one team at the close of each season ends with a loss. There's one reason why we all go through it just for a *chance* to cut down nets: the love of the game. That love drives us to spend the hours on end studying film, scouting, diagramming plays; it's what makes coming to work every day special. The journey.

At UNC Greensboro, "growth" has become the mantra of our program. Younger players improve their skill level; they grow into larger roles. Older players become more vocal; they grow into leadership roles. We reference the saying: "A comfort zone is a beautiful place, but nothing ever grows there." Growth comes with times of adversity, hardship, and discomfort. To be the best coach I can be, I have to stretch myself; I have to get uncomfortable. For our players to grow, they too have to be challenged and pushed. That's the beauty of our culture and how it all works together.

As a player at the University of North Carolina in Chapel Hill, I was surrounded by some of the best players in the country—strong, fast, world-class athletes. I had to find a way to stand out, to earn my way onto the court. I was able to do that by obsessing over the little things that I was coached to do every day: keep my man in front me on defense, feed the post on offense, cut hard, communicate—the not-so-glamorous aspects of the game. I left the alley-oops and behind-the-back passes to my teammates. We won a national championship. To be the last team standing, to cut down nets, is special. That's the ultimate goal.

Victor Solomon, *Church* (detail), 2019

On the other side now as a coach, my perspective has been totally reshaped. I can't control the outcome of a game by shooting the ball, by guarding the other team's best player. I have to figure out a way to put on the court a cohesive group of players who all have the same goals in mind. Our mission is to grow. Outcomes, results, wins/losses—I don't focus on these as much now that I'm on the other side. As a player, that's all that mattered. Now it's the process, the "one day at a time" approach that holds value for me. If we all can get just a *little bit better* every day, the result will take care of itself.

Basketball is a game that brings people together. Teammates become life-long friends. Coaches share a special bond with their players and families. Alma maters are always "home," places to come back to. Banners are ageless—they hang not as a memory, but as a part of history. To go through the ups and downs, the highs and the lows, to "grow" together—that's what makes this game so special.

Suzanne McClelland,
Well Hung (detail), 2004

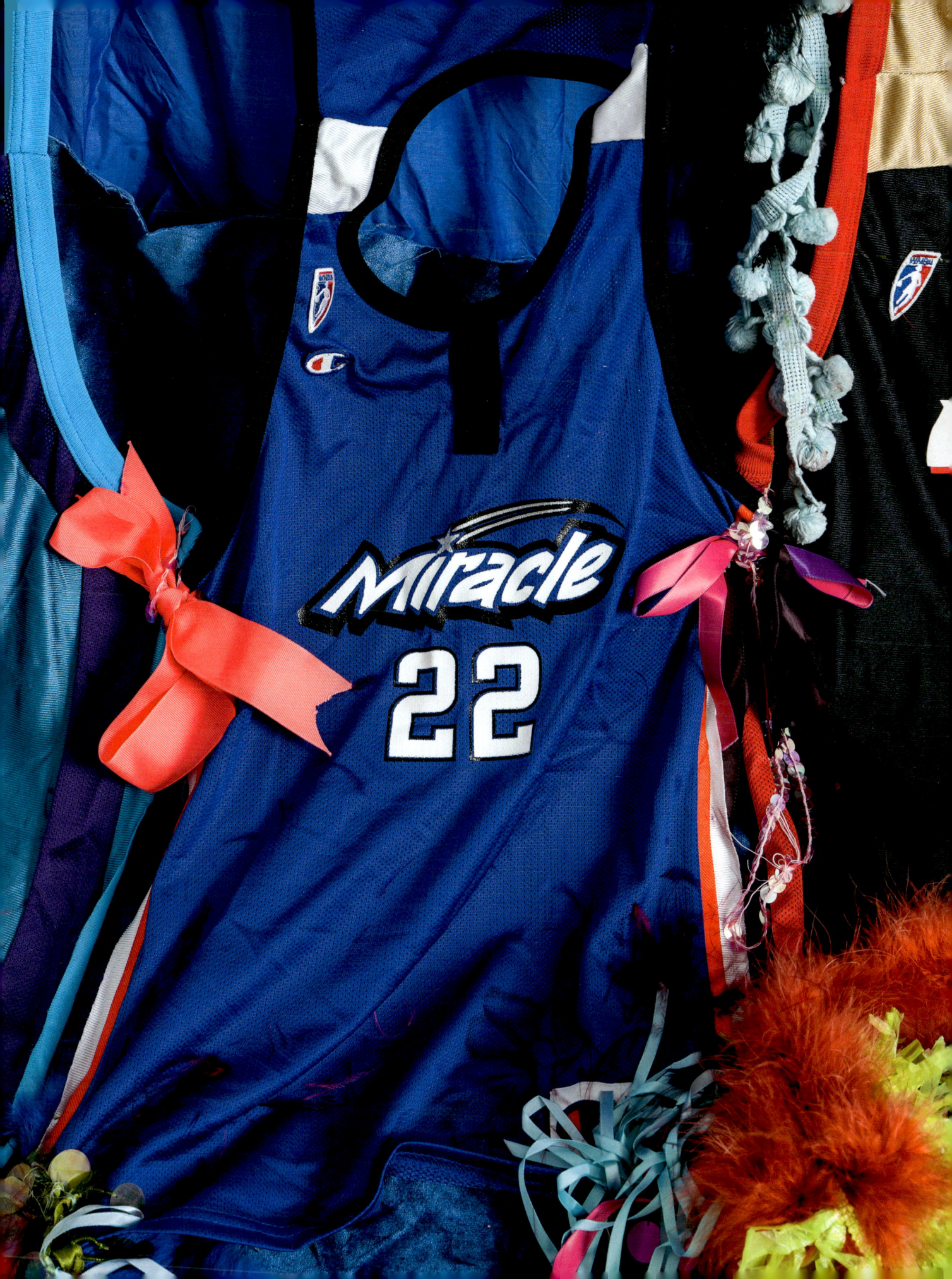

ACKNOWLEDGMENTS

Nancy Doll
Director

My first exposure to any kind of organized basketball was in high school gym class. The girls were divided into two teams. We wore red uniforms and played a version of the game that included multiple guards stationed at circles on the perimeter of the court. My enthusiasm for the game developed later, however, while I lived in Boston and cheered on the Celtics, especially when they played their arch rivals, the Lakers. Now, as a fan of the UNC Greensboro Spartans and director of a museum presenting an exhibition about basketball, it seems things have come full circle.

Before moving to Greensboro, I had little idea that basketball is North Carolina's preeminent sport. Media coverage is given daily to high school, college, and professional teams. One of the first things I was told when I arrived here was that I needed to know who legendary coach Dean Smith was. And I had no idea about the intense rivalry between UNC Chapel Hill and Duke University. I've learned a lot.

First and foremost a game, basketball nonetheless is complicated by a number of underlying issues. My thanks go to the Weatherspoon's Curator of Exhibitions Emily Stamey, who organized *To the Hoop: Basketball and Contemporary Art* for her winning three-point shot in perceptively examining the theme in its myriad layers. I am grateful as well to UNCG's Head Men's Basketball Coach Wes Miller for sharing his insights in the catalogue. Terry Ann R. Neff has shaped the publication with her keen eye and insightful editorial guidance. This book's compelling design is thanks to the publication team at Lucia|Marquand. And, we are delighted to partner with the University of North Carolina Press to make sure the book reaches a wide audience.

The compelling artworks featured in this exhibition and publication are truly the project's starting lineup. And always to be gratefully acknowledged are the artists, galleries, museums, and private collectors who have graciously allowed us to share them with audiences here in North Carolina, as well as in Kansas as the show travels to its second venue.

Every exhibition at the Weatherspoon involves an entire team whose individual contributions are necessary to the show's successful realization. I want to express my gratitude to Ann Grimaldi, curator of education, and Terri Dowell-Dennis, associate curator of education, for organizing meaningful programming around the show. Thanks also to Kim Terbush, registrar, for overseeing the countless details involved with the borrowing and shipping of each loan, and to Alice Culclasure, assistant registrar, for expertly handling all of the image rights and reproductions for the catalogue. Museum preparators Susan Taaffe and Shane Carrico have thoughtfully overseen the installation of each artwork. Loring Mortenson, public relations manager, has promoted the show near and far. Business Manager Valerie McConnell supervised the project's myriad budgetary details, and Development Director Sarah Kathryn Sullivan has successfully helped raise funds to underwrite the project. And, last but not least, Kristen Magod, special assistant for external affairs, has worked with our Weatherspoon Art Museum Advisory Board to create a special celebratory "tip-off" party to launch the show.

It is also a great pleasure to thank those who have provided generous financial support: Sherry Sherrill, Seymour and Carol Cole Levin, Gail Boulton, and Barbara Kretzer have helped to make the exhibition and its related programs possible. In addition, the Jane and John Ellison Publications Endowment has supported this book, support from ArtsGreensboro has aided the show's installation, and funding from the Greensboro Convention & Visitors Bureau will enable us to promote the show widely.

The presentation of *To the Hoop: Basketball and Contemporary Art* at the Weatherspoon coincides with both the ACC and NCAA tournaments being held in Greensboro, affectionately known as "Tournament Town." We hope that the exhibition and this accompanying catalogue engage many new and widespread audiences with the pleasures of the game and the deeper social meanings of what is for many in North Carolina and around the world *the* greatest sport.

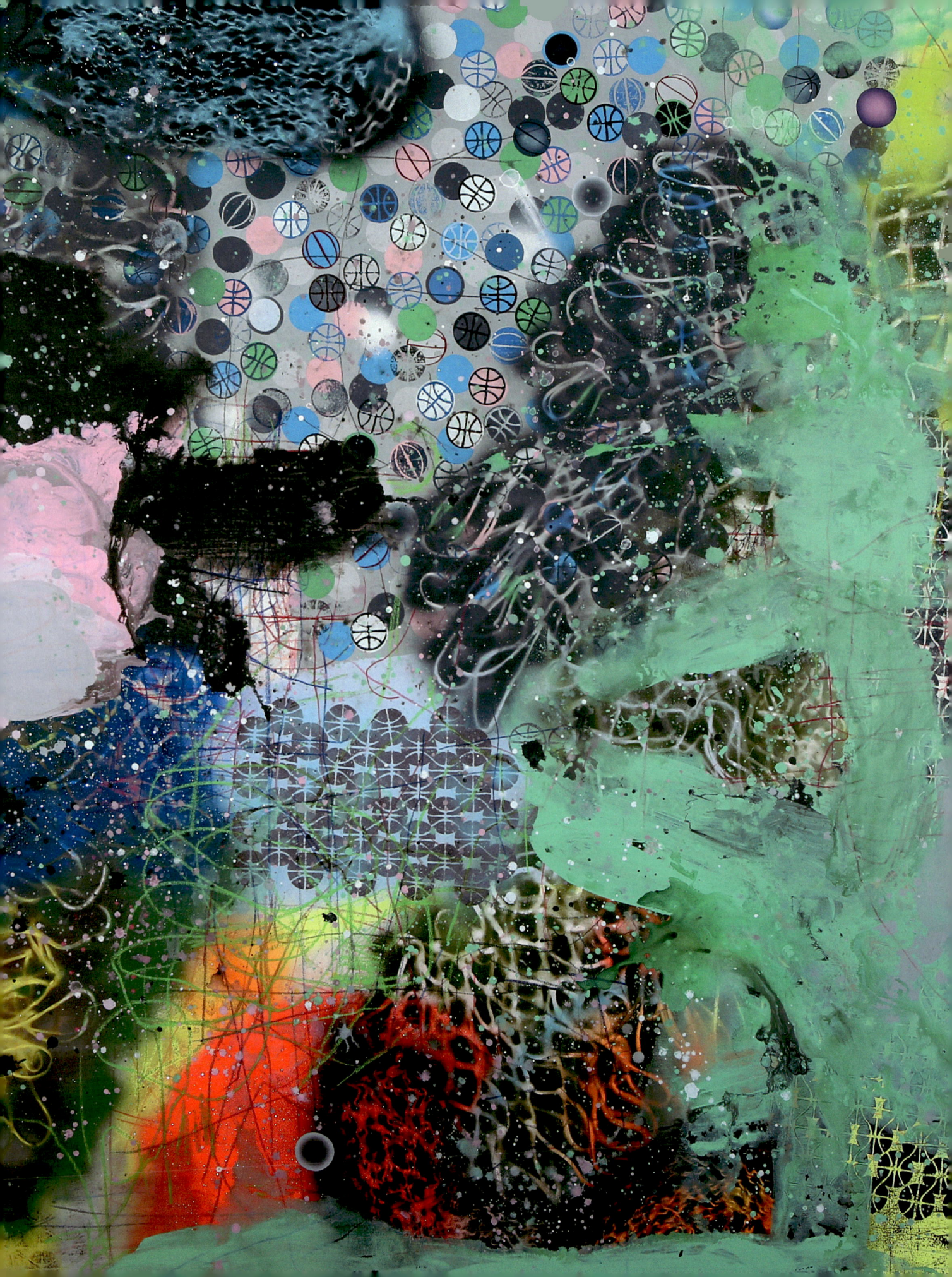

ON THE COURT AND OFF

Emily Stamey
Curator

Beginnings

It started with peach baskets. In 1891 James Naismith, a Canadian theologian and physical education instructor at the Young Men's Christian Association (YMCA) in Springfield, Massachusetts, was asked to devise a recreational activity for restless instructors. Specifically, he was tasked with creating a sport that could be played indoors during the winter months. With two peach baskets, a soccer ball, and a typed list of thirteen rules, he offered basketball. The new game immediately caught on and was quickly refined. Within a few short years, the peach baskets were replaced by a hoop and backboard, and the A. G. Spalding & Bros. company was enlisted to create the first leather basketball.

Within its first half-century, the game's popularity spread as it proved adaptable to different geographic contexts and was embraced by a range of players. In Massachusetts, just a year after its invention, Senda Berenson, an instructor at Smith College, amended the rules for women. Played in YMCAs across the country, the sport spread to both urban and rural locations. In New York City—where space for baseball diamonds and football fields was at a particular premium—it was played not only at the YMCAs, but also at settlement houses serving the city's poorer immigrant communities. Historian Dennis Gildea notes that many of the strongest teams were filled with young Irish and Jewish men.[1]

By 1896 the sport's first professional game was played, and by 1898 its first professional league was formed. In 1904 Edwin Bancroft Henderson, a black gym teacher from Washington, DC, brought the game to segregated high schools in that city,[2] and in 1923 New Yorker Bob Douglas started the first African American professional team, the Harlem Renaissance Big Five—better known as the Rens.[3] In 1936 basketball became an official Olympic sport. Its growing popularity on college campuses led to the establishment of two post-season

David Huffman, *Double Jump* (detail), 2014

1.   Dennis Gildea, "From Basketball to Hoop Heroics: The City Game, 1891 to the Present," in *New York Sports: Glamour, Grit, and the Empire City*, ed. Stephen H. Norwood (Little Rock: University of Arkansas Press, 2018), 153–54.
2.   "Before the NBA Was Integrated, We Had the Black Fives," National Public Radio, March 15, 2014.
3.   Gildea, 155.

collegiate tournaments: the National Invitational Tournament (NIT) in 1938 and the National Collegiate Athletic Association (NCAA) tournament in 1939.

Fast forward some eighty years: today, more people in the United States play basketball than any other sport.[4] The National Basketball Association (NBA) is a multibillion-dollar industry of franchises. Within and beyond its orbit, individual star players have their own brands of shoes and apparel, massive social media followings, and philanthropic foundations. The game has become enmeshed in the music and fashion of hip-hop culture. More than 97 million viewers in the United States watch its college championship, now an iconic event known as "March Madness." Even more viewers follow the tournament from some 180 other countries. Indeed, basketball has spread globally; established in 1932, the International Basketball Federation (FIBA) now counts some 450 million players and fans worldwide.[5]

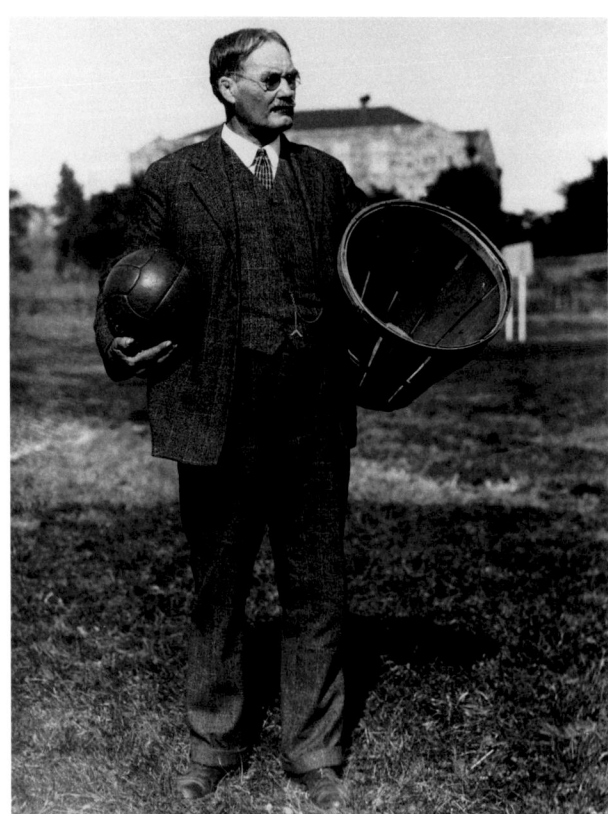

Basketball's Golden Age

Within the game's tremendous growth over the past century, scholars and fans alike note the 1980s and 1990s as its "golden age." In that moment, the game's play literally expanded in significant ways, from the addition of teams to the NCAA tournament to the birth of the Women's National Basketball Association (WNBA). So too, the game's presence grew in terms of recognition, taking on a key role in popular culture.

In part, basketball's growing presence can be credited to television. The game is uniquely suited to TV: It's played at a fast pace in a relatively short amount of time. The action happens on a modest-sized indoor court, where cameras can easily track each pass and shot. Unlike a baseball concealed in a glove or a football buried in a pileup, a basketball is readily seen while in play. So too are the players, who wear shorts and sleeveless jerseys, devoid of helmets or padding. We see their bodies clearly and, thanks to the zoom lens, even their facial expressions.

The Entertainment and Sports Programming Network (ESPN) entered the growing cable television market in 1979, and it quickly made college basketball part of its regular lineup. Suddenly, subscribers could watch back-to-back games played across the country—many of them narrated by colorful

James Naismith invented basketball in 1891 at the International YMCA Training School in Springfield, Massachusetts.

4. "2019 Topline Participation Report" (Silver Spring, Maryland: Sports & Fitness Industry Association, 2019), 30.
5. "2018 International Basketball Migration Report," www.fiba.basketball, accessed online March 13, 2019.

commentator Dick Vitale. Adding to the game's coverage, CBS premiered the NCAA tournament's "Selection Show" in 1982, and then offered $96 million for the rights to broadcast the tournament for the next three years.[6] In 1985 the competition, which had grown from its original eight teams to forty-eight, expanded to sixty-four, transforming the event into a national spectacle. As part of its rituals, even casual followers of the sport would take the blank brackets printed in newspapers and attempt to predict the winning teams.

As college basketball's popularity grew, so too did the professional game's following. As historian Michael Mandelbaum notes, the NBA's success was due in part to the celebrity marketing of its players: "Basketball became a game of stars."[7] Iconic among them were the rival players Magic Johnson of the Los Angeles Lakers and Larry Bird of the Boston Celtics, along with Julius Erving—Dr. J—and Isaiah Thomas. The giant of the era, however, was Michael Jordan, the University of North Carolina player who signed with the Chicago Bulls in 1984 and went on to earn Rookie of the Year, six national titles, and five designations as the NBA's Most Valuable Player, among other achievements. So great was his household name recognition that a 1998 *Time* magazine cover omitted his last name altogether, stating simply "Michael. We may never see his likes again."[8]

Early on in his record-breaking career, Jordan partnered with the Nike shoe company to release the Air Jordan sneaker, a branding deal that would transform sports marketing and align basketball with popular fashion. Throughout the late 1980s and into the 1990s, that alignment grew through the rising popularity of hip-hop culture and basketball's association with it. Sociologist Jeffrey Lane notes, "Uniform designs, team logos, and colors became louder, bigger, brighter, and glossier, mirroring the cut and hues of hip-hop clothing and the shine and gleam of gold rope chains and diamond-covered accessories."[9] A testament to both the sport's popularity and its role in style trends, in 1998 the NBA opened a twenty-five-thousand-square-foot retail store on New York's shopping mecca, Fifth Avenue.

Basketball also loomed large in the world of film. The 1980s and 1990s saw the releases of both critically acclaimed and broadly popular movies featuring the game—from Gene Hackman's classic performance in *Hoosiers* (1986) to Wesley Snipes and Woody Harrelson's comedic dynamism in *White Men Can't Jump* (1992), and from the sobering documentary *Hoop Dreams* (1994) to Warner Brothers' live-action/animation family film *Space Jam* (1996) to Spike Lee's hard-hitting drama *He Got Game* (1998).

6. J. Samuel Walker and Randy Roberts, *The Road to Madness: How the 1973-1974 Season Transformed College Basketball* (Chapel Hill: The University of North Carolina Press, 2016), 146.
7. Michael Mandelbaum, *The Meaning of Sports: Why Americans Watch Baseball, Football, and Basketball and What They See When They Do* (New York: Public Affairs, 2004), 263.
8. *Time* 151, no. 24 (June 22, 1998), cover.
9. Jeffrey Lane, *Under the Boards: The Cultural Revolution in Basketball* (Lincoln: University of Nebraska Press, 2007), 41.

From the silver screen to international broadcasts, basketball also became a global export. With the availability of satellite television, games were aired in more and more countries. By 1996 the NBA championship series was televised in two dozen languages across 175 nations.[10] Basketball's most notable global presence, however, came in the form of the 1992 United States Olympic team, better known as the "Dream Team." Assembled on the heels of professional athletes being allowed in the competition, its roster included eleven superstars—Charles Barkley, Larry Bird, Clyde Drexler, Patrick Ewing, Magic Johnson, Michael Jordan, Karl Malone, Chris Mullin, Scottie Pippen, David Robinson, and John Stockton—plus Duke University's college star Christian Laettner. Greeted by such throngs of fans that its players could not even safely stay in the official Olympic Village, the team went on to play a final gold-medal game that was watched by some 600 million people around the world.[11] So great were the throngs of fans that they drew comparisons with those of Elvis and the Beatles.[12] Basketball—like rock and roll—had reached a pitch of popular appeal.

Art and Basketball Collide

Basketball's crescendo of popularity in the 1980s and 1990s—and with it the ascent of its celebrity stars and marketable brands—coincided with key shifts in the art world, as artists found ways to address and process a culture increasingly filled with media images. Through the 1960s, pop artists such as Andy Warhol and Roy Lichtenstein had emphatically depicted such "low" popular subjects as grocery products, comic-book dramas, and Hollywood celebrities. Their work set the course for a younger generation of artists to expand this attention to consumer culture. Artists working in the 1980s were the first to grow up with a television in the home, and with it a constant stream of advertising. For many of them, the marketing of products and desires became a critical focus, as did ideas of wealth and status—who had them and who did not. Among the many subjects they addressed, basketball began to emerge as a resonant theme.

Throughout the 1980s, and increasingly in the 1990s, artists also took up issues of identity politics. In a world saturated with media images, they considered and critiqued who was represented and who was left out, who was presented positively and who was defined by negative stereotypes. The civil rights movement of the 1960s and the feminist movement of the 1970s had paved the way, and artists carried these social concerns forward as they continued to address the politics of race and gender, as well as sexuality, ethnicity, economics, and globalism. Within this context, basketball was a subject that loomed

10. Mandelbaum, 261.
11. Ibid., 262.
12. Lang Whitaker, "The Dream Team Will Never Die: An Oral History of the Dream Team," *GQ*, June 11, 2012, accessed online March 10, 2019.

large in the popular world of media images and was complexly interwoven with the social issues artists sought to address.

The artworks in this exhibition demonstrate a range of ways in which basketball has been embraced as an artistic subject from the late twentieth century into the present. While some of the works date from basketball's golden age, many more have been made by artists who in those years were impressionable children and teenagers. Their temporal distance provides critical distance as well. Much of their work contains a tension between love of the game and concern over the ways in which it intersects with many things they find troubling in the world. Within the rubric of basketball, one finds numerous themes that extend far beyond sport or entertainment.

Race looms large—specifically representations of African Americans. That focus is not surprising, given the profound visibility of black players in the sport. Among athletes on the NCAA's highly televised Division I men's basketball teams in 2018, 56 percent were black.[13] Within the NBA that same year, more than 73 percent of athletes were black.[14] These figures, and similar ones over the past decades, have been understood in both positive and negative terms. On the one hand, basketball has been seen as a showcase for black talent and success, a particular space of racial acceptance and integration that might encourage the same in the broader social sphere. Conversely, the popular notion of basketball as an arena for black achievement becomes restrictive when it gives way to the stereotype that all black people are good at basketball, and further limiting when basketball is seen as a black person's only means to success. Artists in the exhibition—half of whom are black themselves—have addressed these complex issues of racial representation in myriad ways.

Of course race is not limited to black and white, and artists in the show have also reflected on the game's complicated meanings for other people of color—especially indigenous communities. These artists have considered its historic place in American boarding schools that tried to assimilate Native children into white culture. And they have looked to its current popularity in tribal communities, where players have developed a particularly fast-paced form of play known as "Indian basketball" or "rez ball," and they also see the game as a possible means to leave the reservation on athletic scholarships. That access to education, and with it the idea of making one's way from a place of poverty to a place of wealth, is yet another theme that manifests in popular notions of basketball and in the artworks in this exhibition.

Gender and sexuality also emerge as salient themes. Numerous artists in the exhibition consider the ways in which both masculine and feminine stereotypes

13. NCAA Demographics Database, accessed online March 31, 2018.
14. Richard Lapchi with Brett Estrella, Chelsea Stewart, and Zachary Gerhart, "2018 Racial and Gender Report Card: National Basketball Association" (University of Central Florida: The Institute for Diversity and Ethics in Sport, June 26, 2018), 7, accessed online March 31, 2018. The numbers for WNBA teams were similar, with 78 percent of players identifying as African American.

frame how players are seen and see themselves. These artists ask us to question the monolithic image of the male athlete as strong and straight, hypermasculine and hypersexualized. They also ask us to better acknowledge the fact that women have been competing in basketball since the game was invented, and their long history in the sport is fraught with inverse stereotypes of female players—assumptions that the game's sweat and aggression somehow make a player less of a woman.

In addition to these political themes, philosophical and metaphysical topics emerge. Basketball's association with flight, the way its players seem to defy gravity as they leap and soar, lends itself to considerations of elevation—both spiritual and celestial. Some artists in the exhibition have included references to either Eastern or Western religions and their understandings of states of mind and being that transcend our earthly lives. Others have alluded to the lure of outer space, often visualizing the basketball itself as a planet or star—a distant, beckoning orb.

Writing about the game's allure in a 1985 essay on the NBA, poet Donald Hall noted that part of what mesmerizes us when we watch basketball is the way in which its play is made up of seemingly irreconcilable opposites. He describes the twists, turns, and leaps that set a basketball in motion as "ferocious ballet, gargantuan delicacy, colossal precision."[15] The artworks in this exhibition likewise underscore the conflicting and yet simultaneous ways in which we see the sport: for all the ways in which we can and should examine it through the lens of social concerns, we.can still love the game and relish the seeming magic each time a player soars to the hoop.

15. Donald Hall, "Basketball: The Purest Sport of Bodies," in Donald Hall, *Fathers Playing Catch with Sons: Essays on Sport, Mostly Baseball* (San Francisco: North Point Press, 1985), 158.

THE ARTISTS

Gina Adams

United States (Ojibwa, Lakota, Irish, and
Lithuanian descent), born 1965

Acknowledging both her Native and colonial ancestry, Gina Adams mines histories of cultural preservation and forced assimilation. Within this context, basketball holds both positive and negative associations for the artist. Widely popular today on Native American reservations, the game is often considered a means to higher education and upward mobility. Adams draws attention to the way Native Americans see the sport as a means of being accepted into popular culture no matter where they come from. She also notes that basketball's history in Native communities goes back to the founding of the game itself, and its quick adoption by the late nineteenth- and early twentieth-century boarding schools that forced indigenous students to assimilate to white culture.

Covered with her own hybrid visual vocabulary of designs inspired by those found in Native beadwork, birch bark biting, quill work, and other indigenous mark-making, Adams's ceramic basketballs bear witness to these conflicting associations and invert the boarding schools' aims: instead of overwriting Native youth with white culture, Adams has taken the basketball—a symbol of that culture—and inscribed it with Native motifs. Her choice of material was deliberate: "The ceramic body represents the idea of craft that would have been passed down to me by my ancestors, were their way of life and well-being not purposefully divided and conquered. To ancient people, clay was a means of survival; here I purposely use it to signify survival that continues."[1] Adams also works with historic photographs of Native student athletes—enigmatic images that, despite their documentary nature, raise countless questions. Who are the girls in this picture and what are they thinking? Their expressions are far-ranging: the slightest grin, a wary sidewise glare, a frown, quizzical skepticism, flat stoicism, a defiant scowl. An inscription below identifies them as "BB TEAM 46"; on

1. Gina Adams, artist statement, e-mailed to the author from gallerist Kat Griefen, January 10, 2019.

Honoring Modern Unidentified 27,
Spirit That Remains, 2015
Oil and encaustic on ceramic
9 in. diameter
Courtesy of the artist and
Accola Griefen Fine Art, Brooklyn

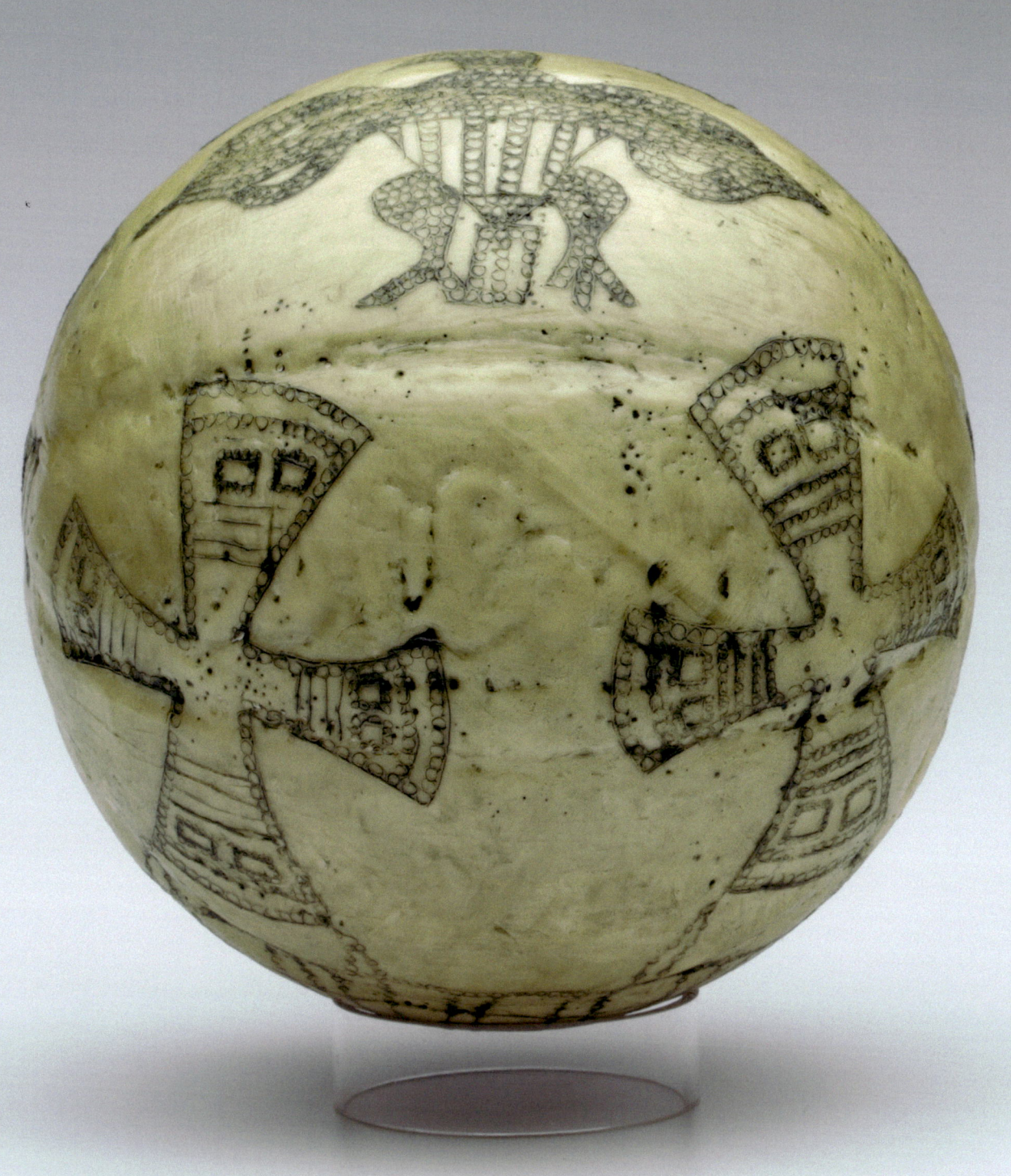

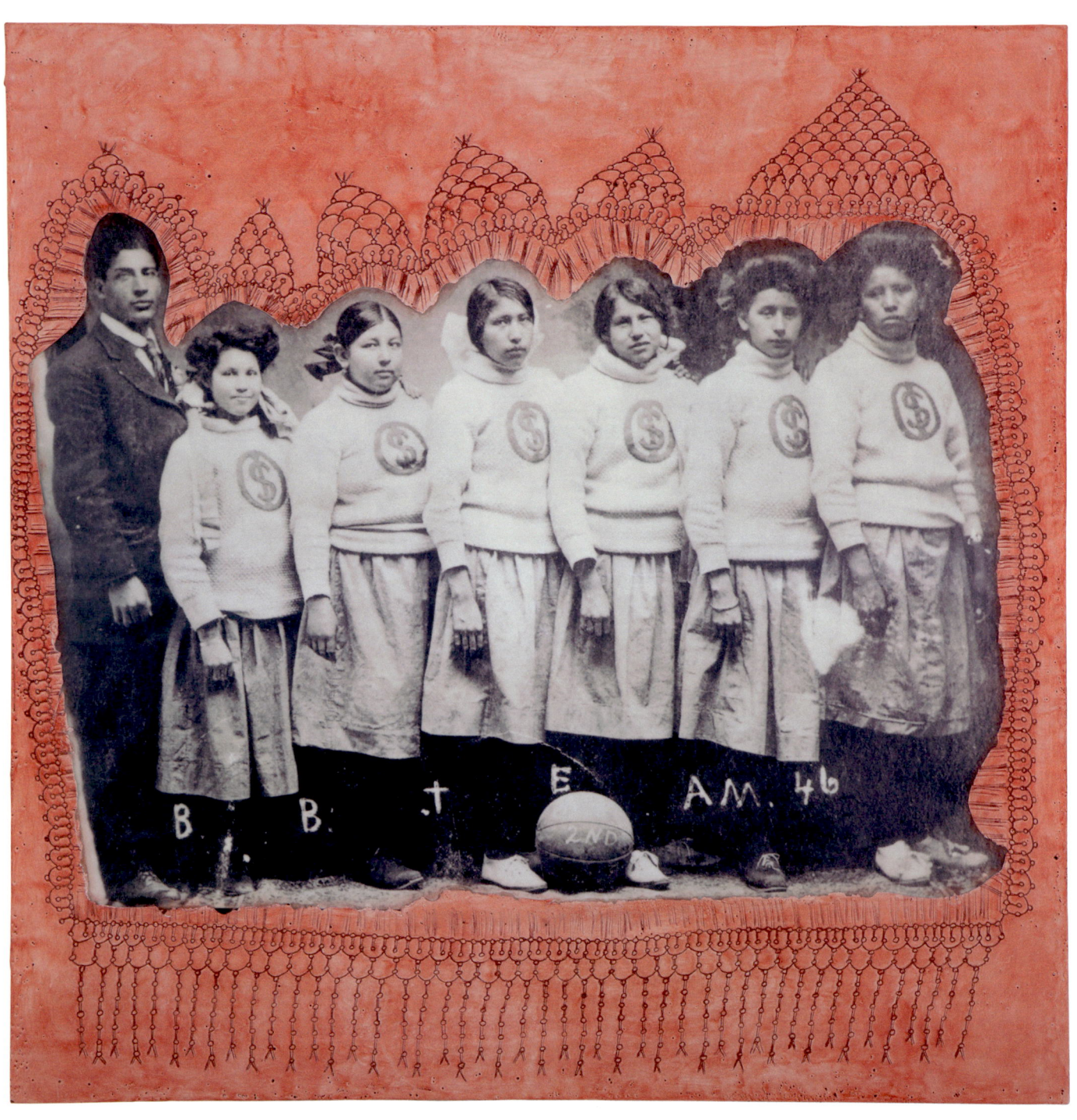

the ball at their feet, a "2ND" suggests that perhaps they have just placed in a tournament. Adams found the photograph in the University of Oklahoma libraries, one of many historic images of Native peoples with no accompanying documentation.

The entwined O and S on the girls' sweaters stands for Osage, an Indian Nation whose reservation is located in northwest Oklahoma.[2] The style of their uniforms and broad hair bows suggests the image dates from the 1910s—a period following the community's forced migration to Oklahoma in the 1870s and bracketed by the terror visited on it in the 1920s by white murderers jealous of its oil wealth. Adams layered the image with wax pigmented blood red, explaining: "I wanted [the image] to have the feeling as if an upper layer had been peeled away to reveal the photograph. In this lifted layer, it was my wish to have the edges feel torn, thus to signify exposing the memory of an actual event."[3] She incised the wax with scallops and dots inspired by beadwork patterns from her own Ojibwa heritage. In both the ceramic basketball and the altered found photograph, Adams honors Native culture and the individuals—past and present—who struggle to maintain and celebrate their Native identity.

Girls Native American Indian Basketball Team I, 2016
Photograph, oil, and encaustic
30 × 30 in.
Courtesy of the artist and
Accola Griefen Fine Art, Brooklyn

2. Ibid. Adams received permission from the Oklahoma Historical Society to work with this image.
3. Ibid.

Daniel Arsham

United States, born 1980

I n sculptures that comprise a sort of fictional archaeology, Daniel Arsham transports viewers to imagined futures where we examine relics of our present. Cast from geologic materials, his forms are both familiar and foreign, rendered with exacting detail yet intentionally cracked and crumbled to suggest the wear of time. Sports equipment, jerseys, and shoes are frequent finds among these artifacts, especially those associated with basketball. As Arsham notes, "Basketballs are something that people recognize in terms of culture and even know what the texture feels like."[1] We associate the ball with teams, players, brands, and abstract notions about competition and success, but many of us also have held basketballs and retain nostalgic tactile memories from gymnasiums, playgrounds, or driveways of our youth.

To see blue basketballs in crystallized, fractured form disrupts their meaning. Here, the balls are cast from hydrostone—a calcium sulfate–based plaster—and varying amounts of blue calcite. They are arranged from dark to light on a custom-built cart that recalls both a basketball rack and laboratory shelving. Rather than playthings at the ready, they resemble specimens for examination, prohibited from functionality by their sheer weight. It is a cautionary tale: What will become of today's most famed basketball stars and sporting brands? Will the game itself be as popular in the future as it is now? And, perhaps more broadly, which aspects of our culture will fade and which will endure? Constantly experimenting with new materials, Arsham has made a new rack of basketballs for *To the Hoop*, this time in gradient shades of violet, cast with purple amethyst.

"Basketballs are something that people recognize in terms of culture and even know what the texture feels like."

1. Daniel Arsham, statement in *Fictional Archaeology: Daniel Arsham* (New York: Galerie Perrotin, 2015), n.p.

Blue Calcite Gradient Basketballs, 2016
Blue calcite crystal, hydrostone, and powder-coated steel stand
50 ³/₈ × 39 ¹⁵/₁₆ × 15 ¹⁵/₁₆ in.
Courtesy of the artist and Perrotin, New York

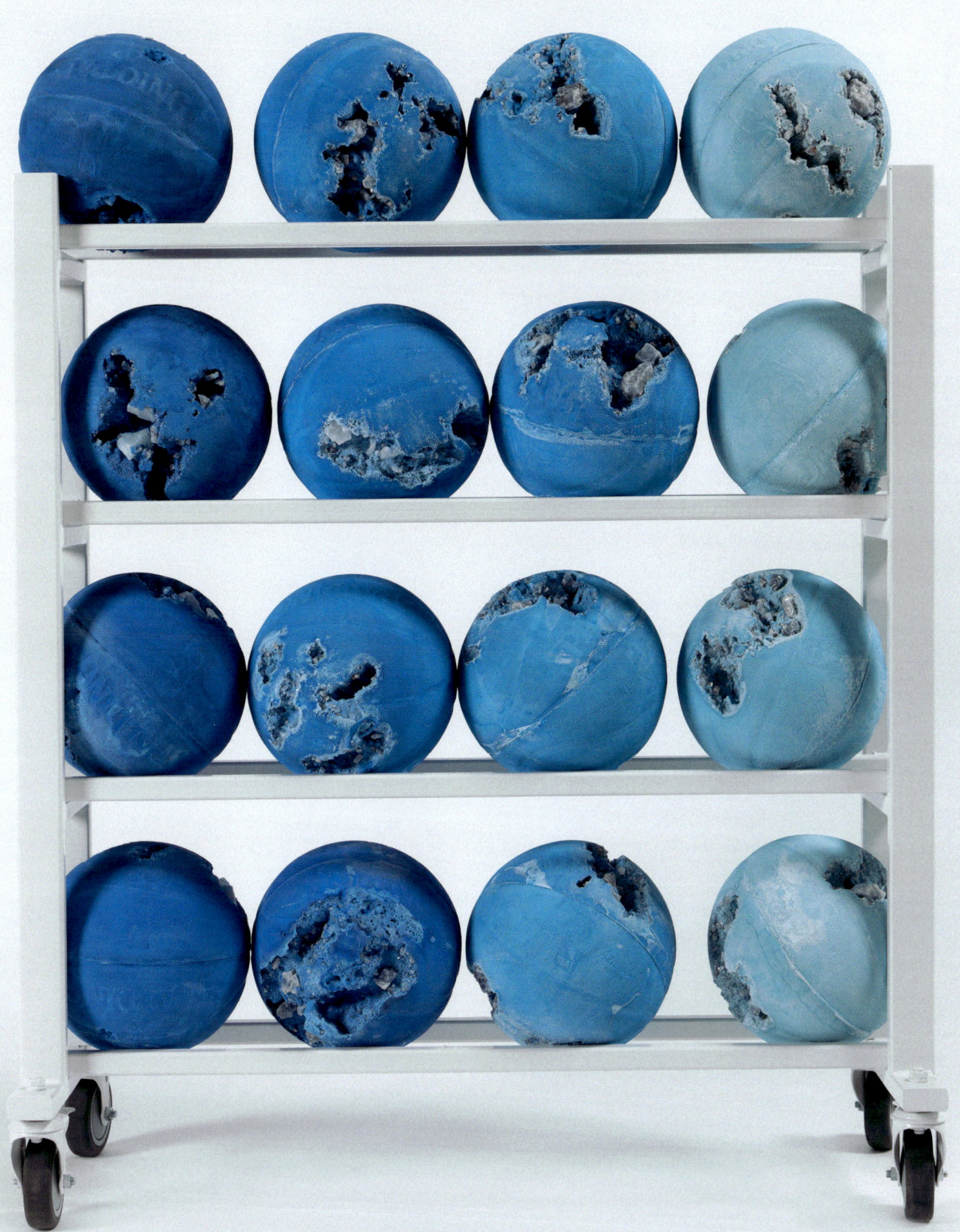

Bill Bamberger

United States, born 1956

Bill Bamberger's photographs of outdoor basketball hoops across the country and around the world underscore the popularity of a game that is relatively simple in its structure. One needs only a ball and a hoop to play basketball. The hoop may or may not have a net or a backboard. It might be suspended above painted asphalt or a bare patch of ground. Whether set against the rural backdrop of a cotton field, a row of houses in a suburban neighborhood, or a painted mural in the city, every hoop Bamberger photographs, although absent people, stands as a marker of human presence. These quiet images of hoops evoke the players who have used them—alone or in groups, recently or long ago. Their invisible presences activate each space. Each individual image suggests a particular story. Taken together, the series—thousands in total—highlights the universality of a game that is played by rich and poor, formally and informally, in countless geographic locations.

A native Philadelphian, Bamberger grew up playing basketball on schoolyard courts. Describing the origins of this photographic series and its ongoing vibrancy, he has said: "A photograph of someone making a great shot or a great move takes place in a fraction of a second, but a photograph of that same court taken without people is about a period of time in the layered history of a place. It is about the people who played on that court, who built that community, many of whom have come and gone." Begun in 2004, Bamberger's project is now international in scope, encompassing hoops in locations ranging from Jamaica to Rwanda, Guatemala to Italy, Mexico to Namibia—a testimony to the game's now global popularity.

"A photograph of someone making a great shot or a great move takes place in a fraction of a second, but a photograph of that same court taken without people is about a period of time in the layered history of a place."

Farm Home by Cotton Field, Plymouth, North Carolina, 2004
Color inkjet print
19 5/16 × 28 7/8 in.
Edition
Courtesy of the artist

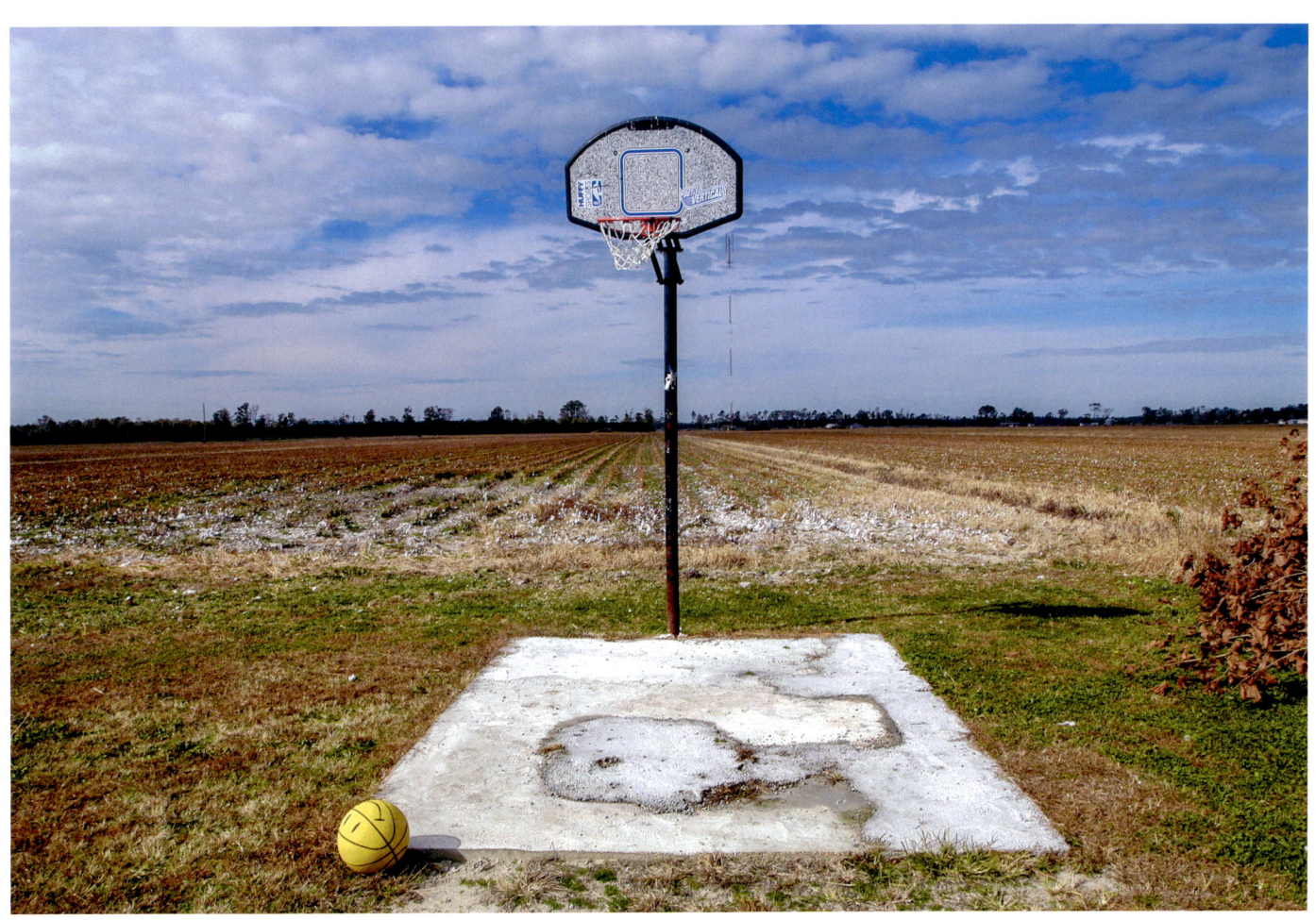

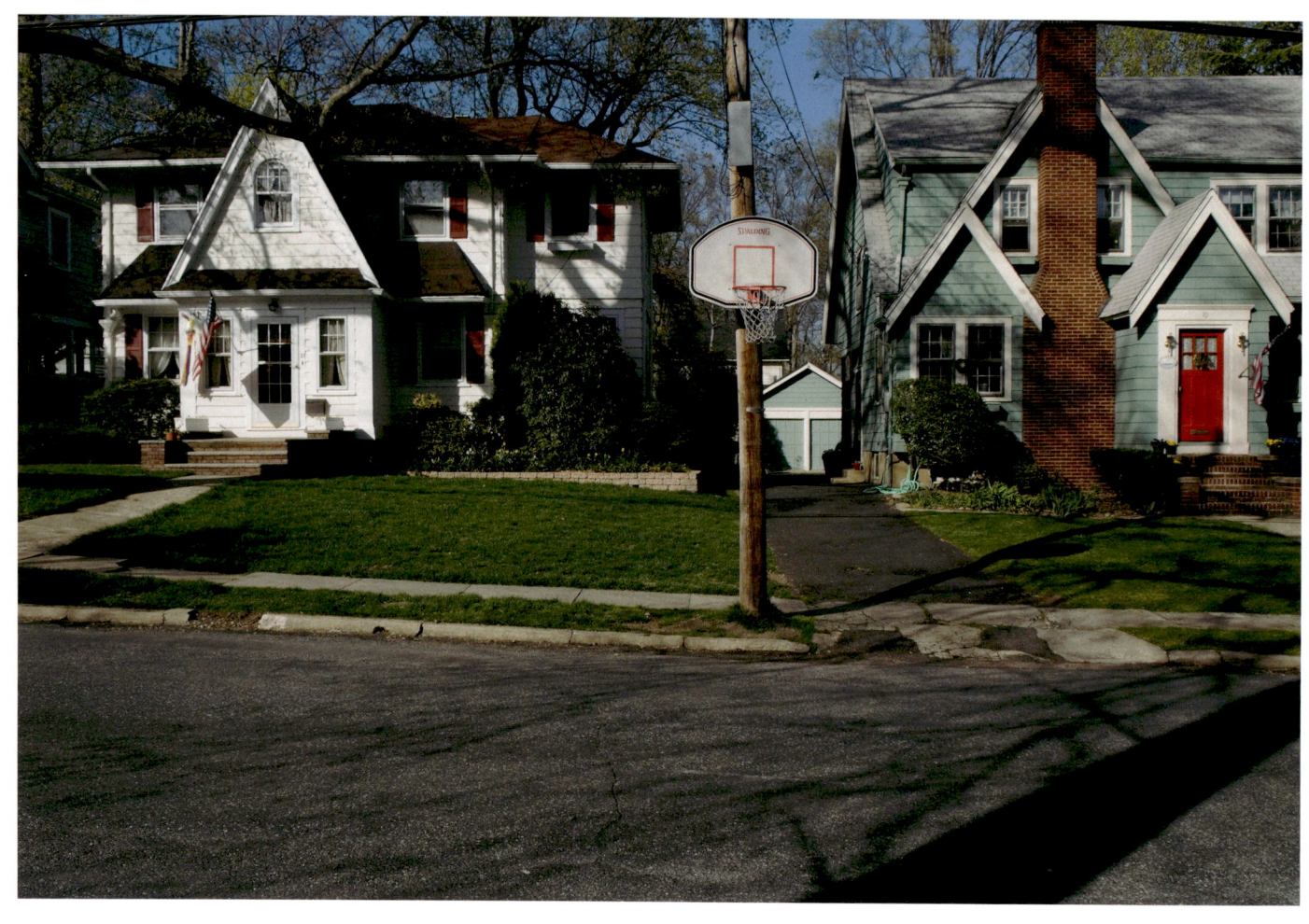

Suburban Neighborhood,
Millburn, New Jersey, 2006
Color inkjet print
19 ⁵/₁₆ × 28 ⁷/₈ in.
Edition
Courtesy of the artist

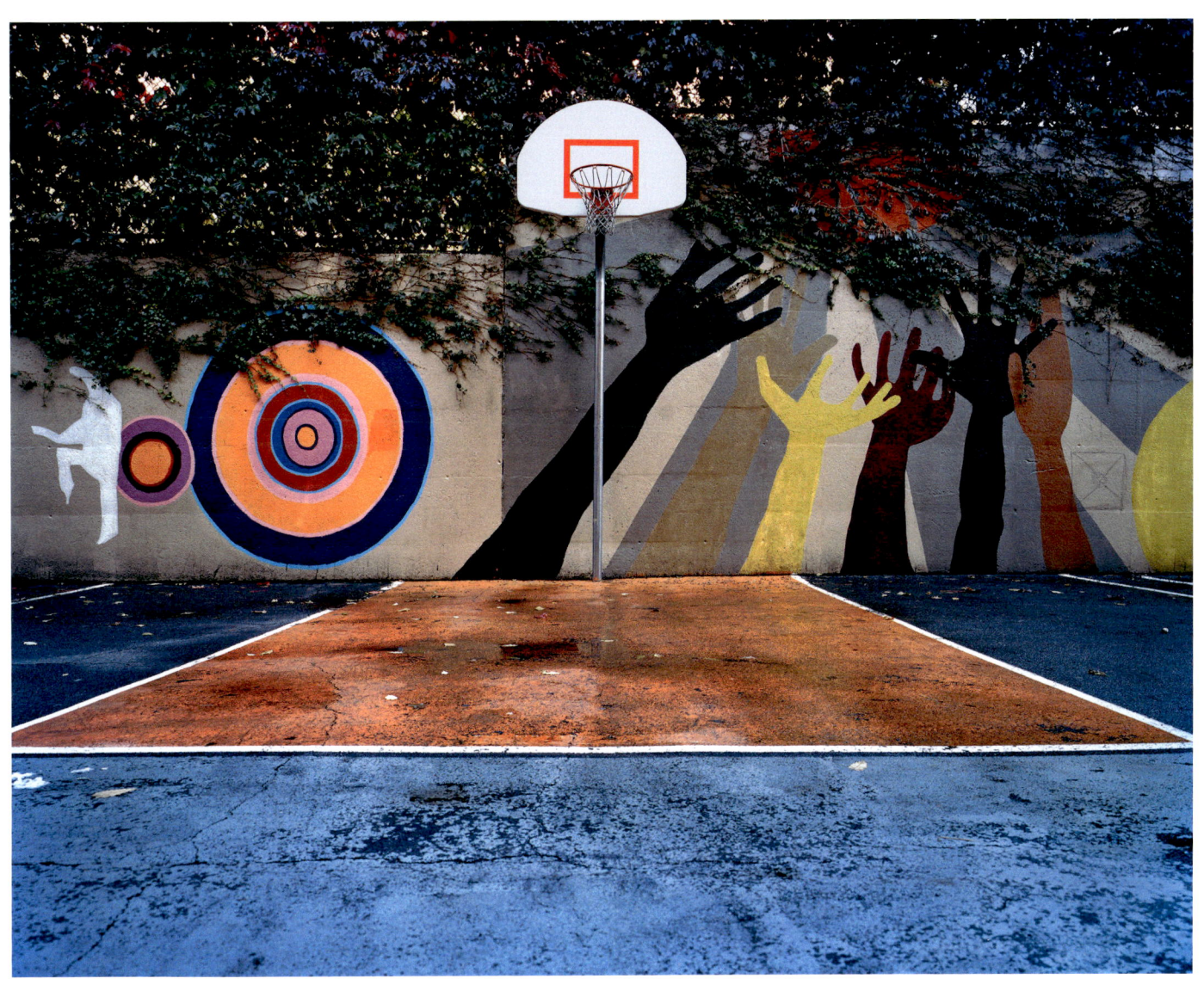

Charter School Playground,
Harlem, New York, 2007
Color inkjet print
22 ½ × 28 ⅝ in.
Edition
Courtesy of the artist

Janet Biggs

United States, born 1959

With its title referring simultaneously to the artwork's format and subject, Janet Biggs's video installation *One-on-One* features stark juxtapositions. Projected horizontally across the wall is a 360-degree pan of a vacant arena, the dizzying view intensified by a musical track featuring a steady bassline and increasingly fast-paced guitar riffs. Projected vertically on a screen in the center of the room is a scene of two female basketball players locked in a dynamic struggle for the ball. Their battle is accompanied by the sound of that ball being dribbled and their shoes squeaking on the floor. Dressed in the familiar pairing of white "home" and colored "away" uniforms, the players appear to be from different teams. But, in fact, both women wear University of Connecticut jerseys: they are teammates, Morgan Valley and Maria Conlon, practicing against one another and vying for individual control in order to later play as one. Biggs recalls that in working with the athletes she was struck by how they occupied a space caught between "extreme aggression and beautiful dance."[1] So often, we consider aggression to be masculine and dance feminine. Given those stereotypes, Biggs notes, "Sports is a socially acceptable way of changing gender roles."

Viewing these two scenes together, we can imagine the arena seats filled with thousands of fans watching the players compete. How emotionally invested will the crowd become? Will the players, focused on the game, even be aware of the audience? Would they play as fiercely if no one watched? By simultaneously isolating and overlapping constituent elements of a basketball game, Biggs probes questions of power, performance, and spectatorship.

> ## "Sports is a socially acceptable way of changing gender roles."

1. Janet Biggs, quoted in L. P. Streitfeld, "The Power of UConn's Women on Display," *Hartford Courant*, December 2, 2004, accessed online via jbiggs.com April 12, 2019.

One-on-One, 2004
Two-channel video
installation with sound
(channel #1) 8 min. 55 sec. loop;
(channel #2) 30 sec. loop
Courtesy of the artist and
Cristin Tierney Gallery, New York

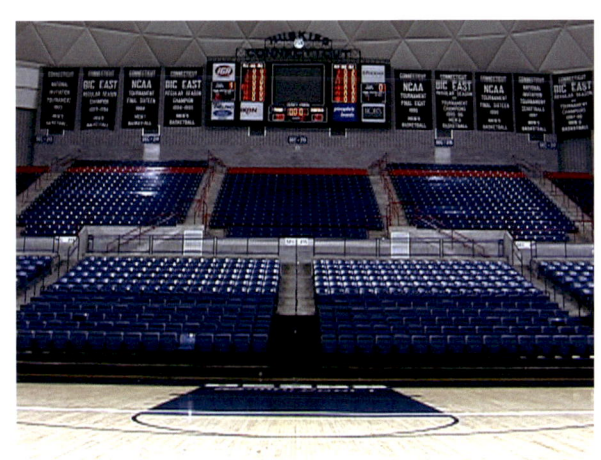

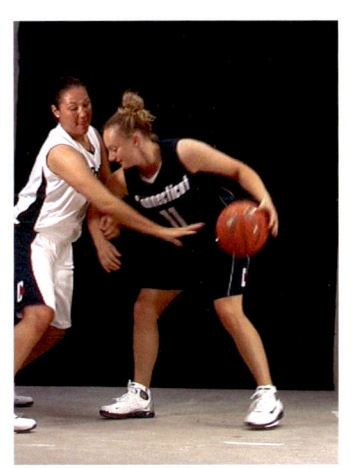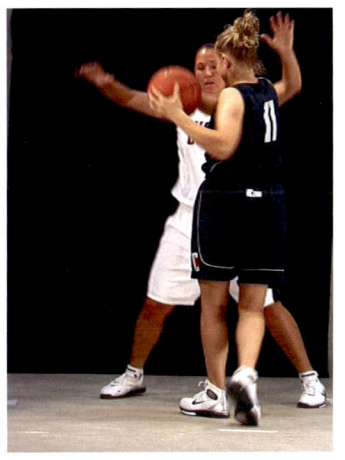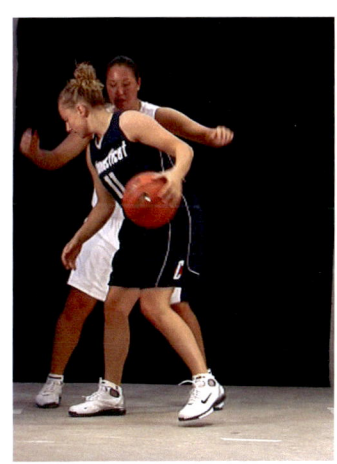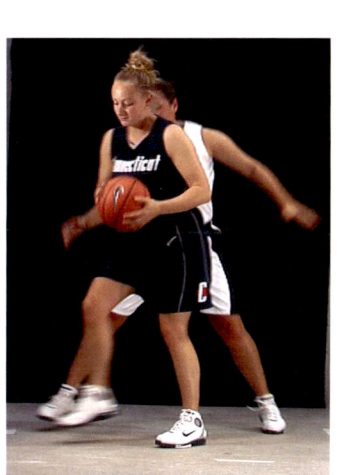

Mark Bradford

United States, born 1961

Standing six feet, eight inches tall by the time he was fifteen years old, Mark Bradford was frequently told he should be a basketball player. Instead, he became an artist—but sports are a recurrent theme in his work. "Practice" is a term with currency in both realms. As an art-world noun, it describes an artist's overall application of ideas and methods; as a sports verb, it signals the action of repetitively perfecting skills. In this video, Bradford merges the two meanings by applying artistic metaphor to the physical act of dribbling a ball and taking shots.

For his performance, Bradford crafted an oversized hoop skirt in the purple and gold of his hometown team, the Los Angeles Lakers. Hampered by its monumental lengths of fabric as they catch under his feet and float in the wind, he falls, rolls, gets back up, and tries again to maintain control of both his body and the ball. He explained *Practice*: "It was about road blocks, on every level, cultural, gender, racial . . . Regardless that they are there, you keep going. It is important to continue . . . I always make the shot; sometimes it takes me a little longer to get there, but I always make the shot."[1] That idea of perseverance and ultimate triumph might be considered more broadly as signaled by the dress itself. Its skirt recalls the antebellum period in which a black man such as Bradford would likely have been enslaved. The basketball jersey bodice suggests the contemporary stereotype that all black men play the game, and play it well. The dress as a whole becomes a metaphor for the sweep of American history and the ongoing struggles of so many individuals to break free of stereotypes.

"It was about road blocks, on every level, cultural, gender, racial . . . Regardless that they are there, you keep going. It is important to continue . . . I always make the shot; sometimes it takes me a little longer to get there, but I always make the shot."

1. Mark Bradford, as stated in "Mark Bradford: Art21 Preview from Season 4 of 'Art in the Twenty-First Century'" (Art21, 2007) accessed via YouTube, https://www.youtube.com/watch?v=rM3x0XOll30, February 20, 2019.

Practice, 2003
Single-channel color video
with sound, 3 min.
Edition
Collection of Laura Lee Brown and
Steve Wilson, 21c Museum Hotels

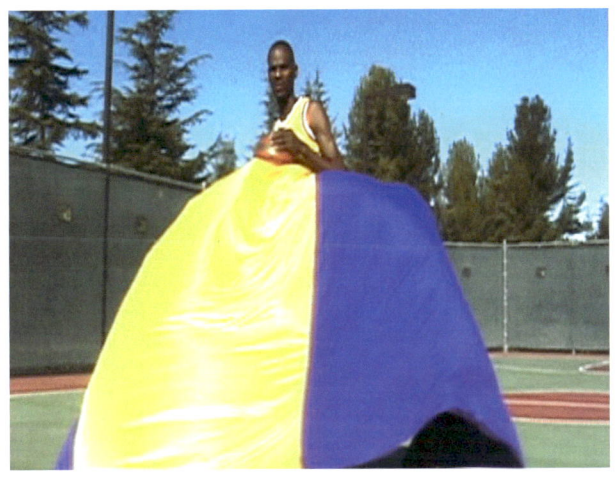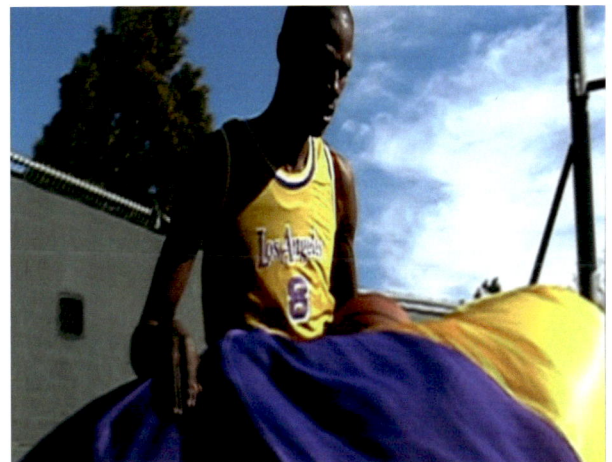
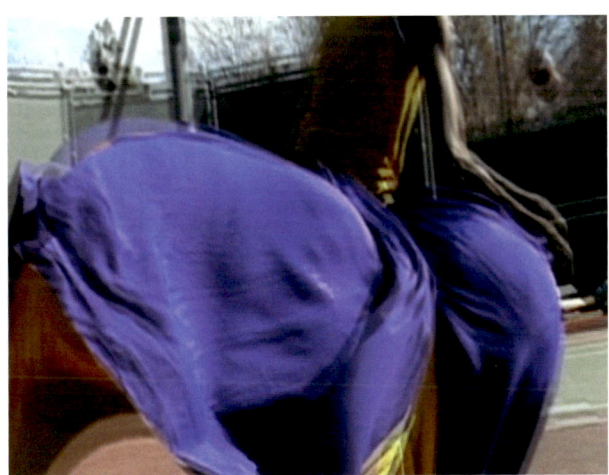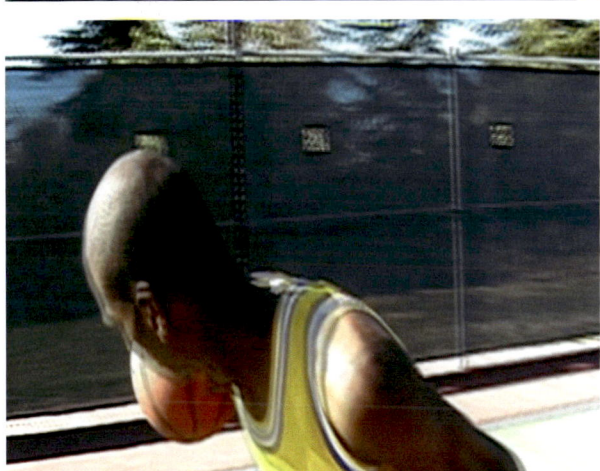
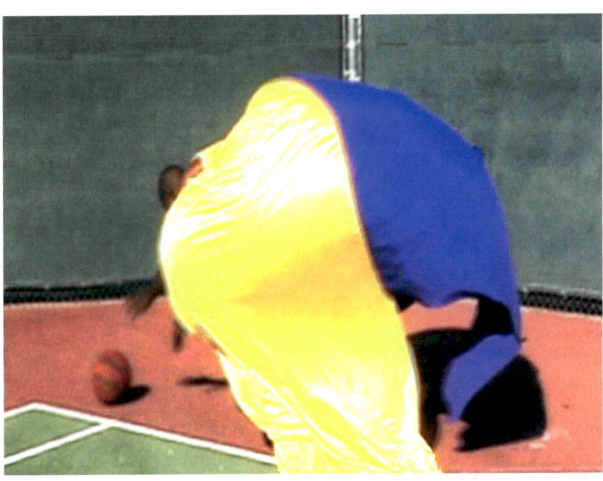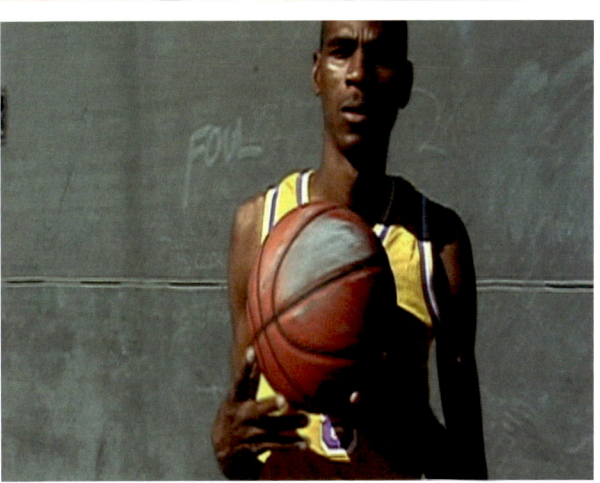

Kendell Carter

United States, born 1970

with photographer Dawn Altier

United States, born 1978

On a bluff overlooking the Pacific Ocean, artist Kendell Carter sits with his head slightly bowed, hands resting on his knees. The pose is one traditionally used for meditation: crossed legs a grounding foundation, lowered head a reminder to mentally focus inward, and hands upturned in a gesture of acceptance. Carter's composition—framing himself between the sloping contours of the shoreline with a calm expanse of sea and sky beyond—is familiar, recalling any number of advertisements for meditation retreats or wellness centers. Unexpected, however, is the basketball jersey that he wears—an article of clothing we associate with a starkly different context of fast-paced play on an indoor court, bright lights, and a cacophonous roar of cheers, yells, buzzers, music, squeaking shoes, and the thump of a ball.

In the sharp contrast between these two scenes—the pictured tranquility and the imagined competition—lies the tension that interests Carter. In all his work, he seeks to reward imaginative moves beyond clichés and stereotypes. Describing this image, he notes, "It's an alternative to the idea of the physically heroic male athlete" whose success rests in physical strength and individual dominance. He wears the jersey of legendary player Scottie Pippen, famed not only for his individual skills but for his collaborative play with fellow Chicago Bull Michael Jordan. Pippen and Jordan were coached by Phil Jackson, nicknamed the "Zen Master" for his use of team meditation. This jersey, however, is not Pippen's number 33 in Bulls' red, but rather the uniform he wore for the United States' historic "Dream Team" at the 1992 Olympic Games. Composed entirely of superstars, that team was remarkable not for any one player but for their astonishing collective and cooperative skill.

> **"It's an alternative to the idea of the physically heroic male athlete"**

*Meditation on Team
(Waves for Scottie)*, 2017
Color Duratran photograph and lightbox
36 × 48 × 5 in.
Edition
Courtesy of the artists and
Edward Cella Art & Architecture,
Los Angeles

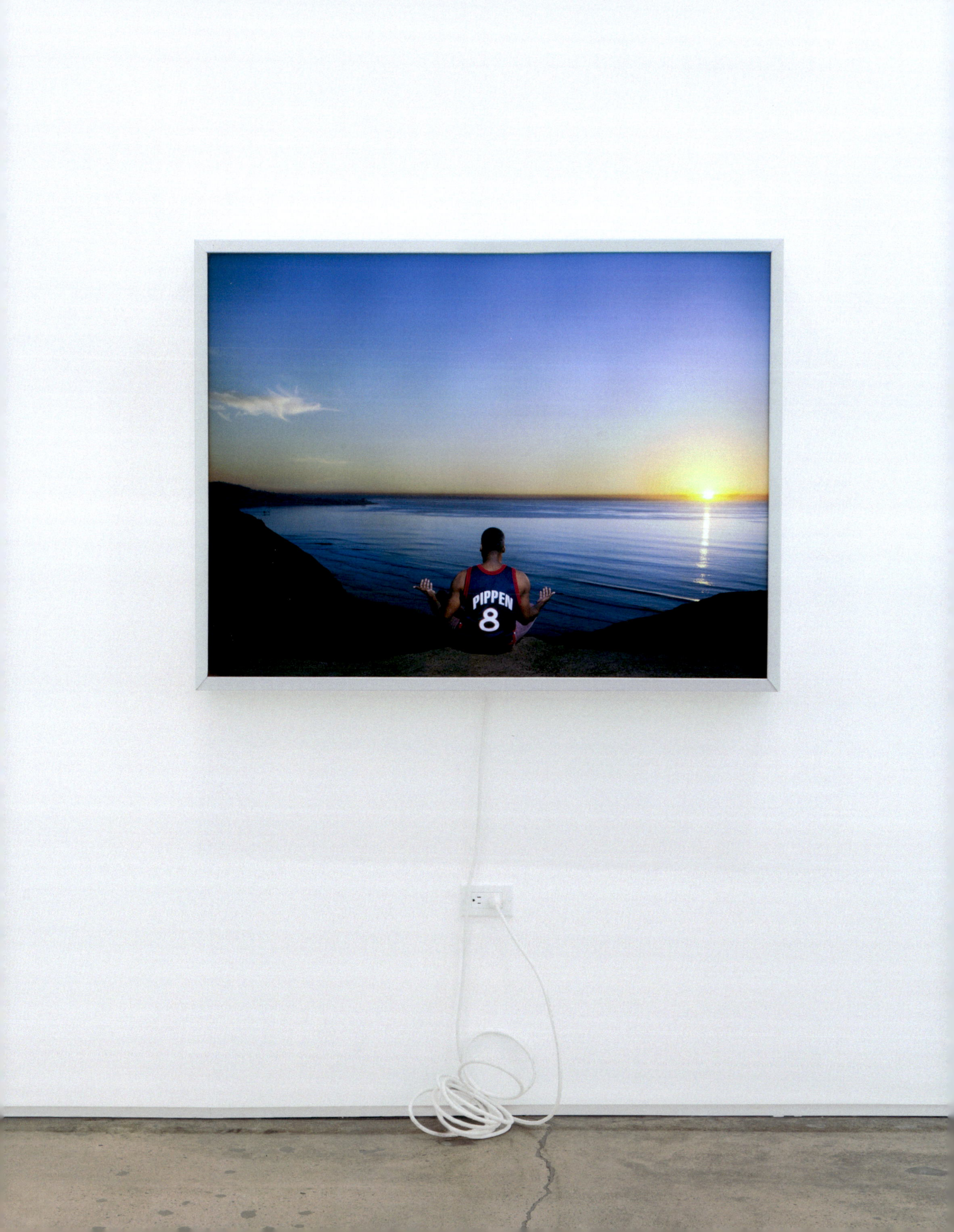

André Leon Gray

United States, born 1969

Using discarded objects, André Leon Gray crafts assemblages that speak to his interests in spirituality, philosophy, and black culture. Intended to evoke an African mask, *Black Magic (It's Fantastic)* presents a fierce visage—its cowrie-shell eyes bulging, painted teeth bared, and features framed by a mane of red shoelaces. The artist describes the artwork's title as "a play on the way some people see sports almost like a religion."[1] Indeed, the rituals involved with attending a basketball game—the elaborate presentation of the starting line-up, the call and response of cheers, the dramatic use of music—hold significant parallels with a range of spiritual ceremonies across different religions.

In this sculpture, Gray also comments on the desires for power and achievement that are a part of competitive sports. Crowning the figure's head with a basketball—from which the bristles of a street sweeper's brush radiate like sunbeams—creates a heraldic aura. Gray considers how players vie for titles—champion, most valuable player—that will transform them into stars. Beneath the sunburst, carefully placed rhinestones form a stylized basketball in which the grip lines are tipped like arrows, making them into compass points that suggest movement, perhaps the quest for achievement and recognition. The larger design of which that form is a part is inspired by a Haitian *veve*, a drawing used in Vodou ceremonies to invite the presence of divine spirits. On the mask's headband hovers one of basketball's most celebrated "spirits," the iconic leaping silhouette of Michael Jordan.

> " . . . some people see sports almost like a religion."

Black Magic (It's Fantastic), 2005
Acrylic, rhinestones, basketball, braided synthetic hair, street sweeper brush, shoelaces, headband, miniature clay pots, wood, and cowrie shells on wood ironing board
67 × 31 × 9 ½ in.
North Carolina Museum of Art, Raleigh, Purchased with funds from the Friends of African and African American Art, and with additional funds provided by North Carolina Mutual Life Insurance Company

1. André Leon Gray, as stated in the video description "Black Magic (It's Fantastic)," NCMA Learn, https://learn.ncartmuseum.org /resources/black-magic-its-fantastic-by-andre-leon-gray/, accessed February 24, 2019.

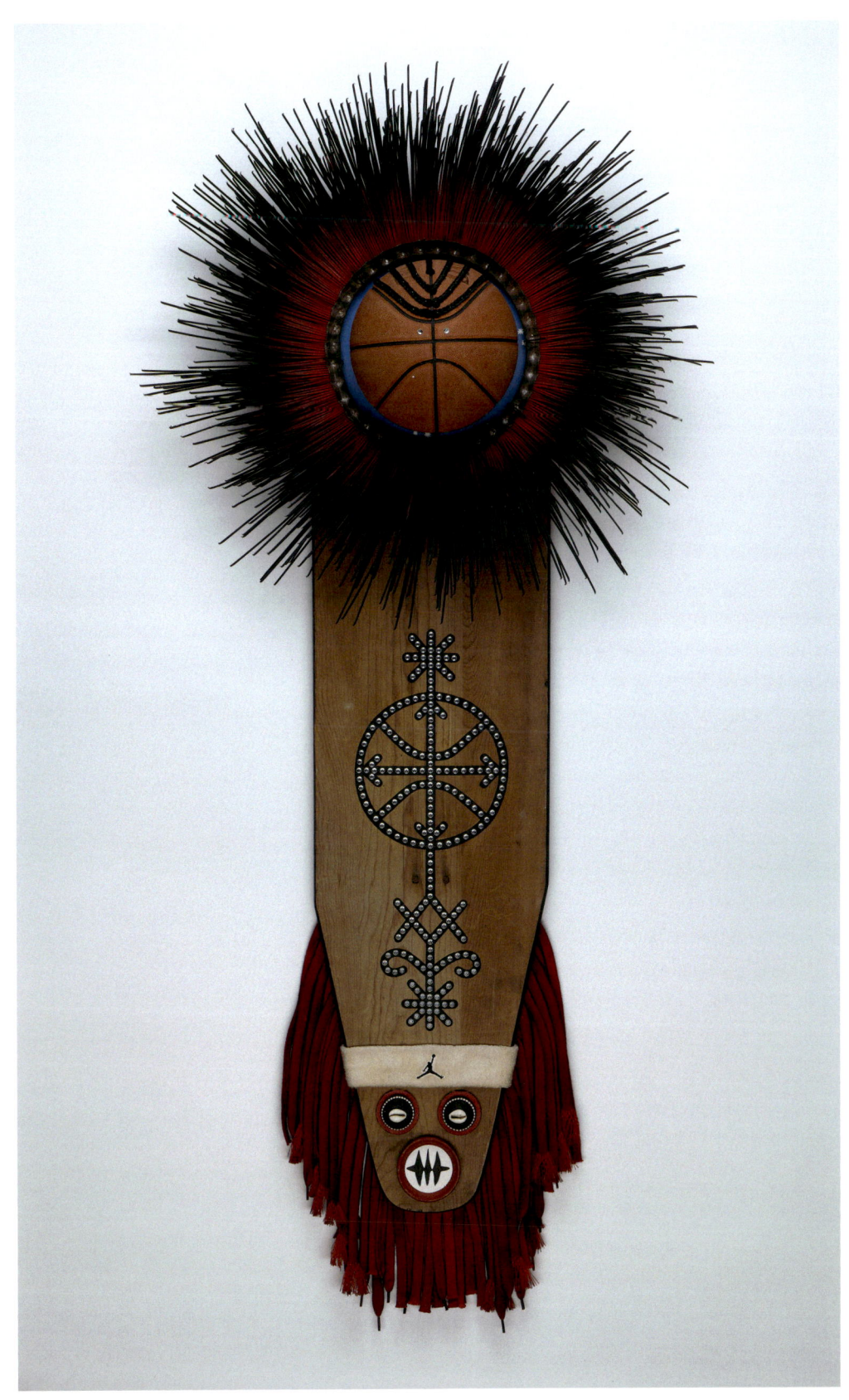

David Hammons

United States, born 1943

David Hammons is best known for using humble materials and a sharp sense of humor to create sculptures that speak to black experiences. Working in Harlem in the 1980s, he created ephemeral works of art made from such ordinary detritus as bottles and food scraps. Many of his projects were inspired by the numerous makeshift basketball hoops he found throughout the neighborhood—rigged from paper bags, cardboard boxes, and wooden crates. Troubled by the emphasis placed on the game for black youth, Hammons stated, "Basketball has become a problem in the black community because kids aren't getting an education. They're pawns in someone else's game . . . you should have higher goals in life than basketball."[1]

Hammons also recorded his convictions in photographs. In this image, made while traveling in the South, he documented a found hoop for the magazine *Parkett*. He additionally provided the caption for the image: "Readymade magic. A basketball hoop fashioned from the rim of a bicycle tire, embedded in a living tree in a Charleston backyard, testifies to the ingenuity of its anonymous maker."[2] That laudable description is countered by the artist's sarcastic title for the photograph, *Money Tree*—an allusion to fabled riches that the construction is unlikely to yield. The hoop sags and the uneven, grassy ground below is less than ideal for running or dribbling. It seems doubtful that practicing here will lead to a lucrative sports career.

Money Tree, 1992
Sepia print
16 ⅛ × 10 ⅞ in.
Edition
Nasher Museum of Art, Duke University, Durham, North Carolina, Gift of Blake Byrne, 2017.4.7

1. Merrell Noden, "A Very High Form of Art," *Sports Illustrated*, December 24, 1990: 14.
2. David Hammons, "Money Tree," edition for *Parkett* 31 (1992); description accessed online via parkettart.com, April 12, 2019.

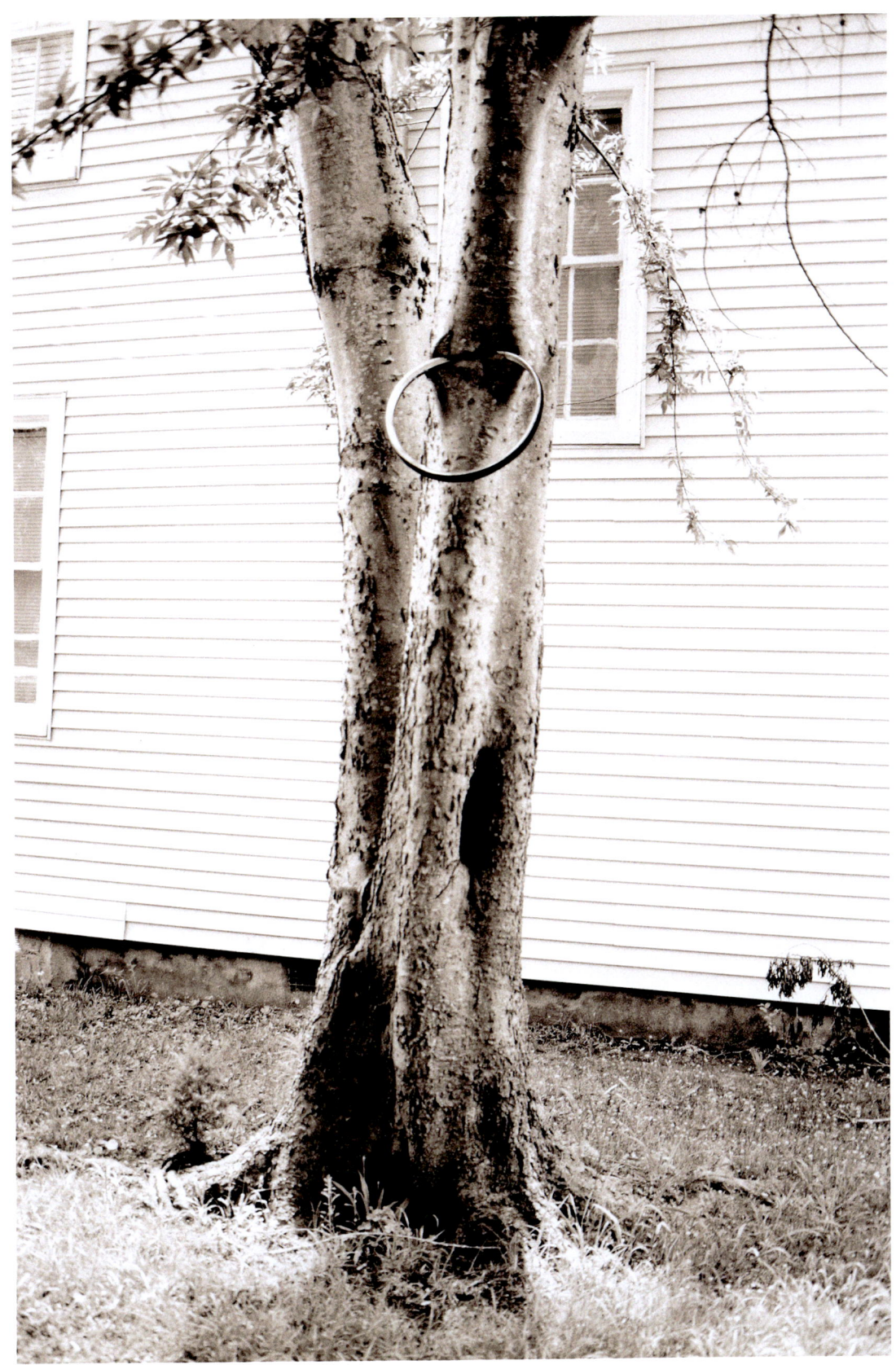

David Hilliard

United States, born 1964

David Hilliard sequences single photographs to construct multipart panoramas in which the shifts of focus heighten the narrative potential. In this triptych of boys on a basketball court, there is a distinct tension between balance and imbalance, stasis and motion. In the middle image, both the ceiling beam and the half court line emphasize the composition's center, but the alignment is not exact. Rather than anchor the image, these elements cause it to tilt. The shirtless "skins" at the center of the court are framed relatively evenly in the foreground by the "shirts." The numbers on the jerseys of the boys at the inside of the flanking panels, 32 and 23, appear as mirror images of one another, providing further balance, yet, as with the center line, the equilibrium is upset by the seemingly doubled appearance of player 32.

Hilliard's subjects and the tensions with which he imbues them are often tied to his personal experiences, among them his early struggles coming to terms with his gay identity. Describing his interest in photographing these young men on a basketball court, he has recounted that in his own youth he intensely disliked gym classes and was always extremely uncomfortable when told to remove his shirt to play "shirts versus skins."[1] Although the boys in this image strike defiant stances—hands on hips or arms crossed—and the text painted on the wall above them declares the space the "Home of the Warriors," we have no way to assess their own comfort level in this situation.

1. Alex Pure, "Photographer David Hilliard Focuses on Motivation in Visiting Artist Lecture," *Hamilton News & Events*, November 14, 2008, accessed online April 12, 2019.

Shirts vs. Skins, 2001
Archival pigment print
Three parts, each 40 × 30 in.
Edition
Courtesy of the artist and
Yancey Richardson Gallery, New York

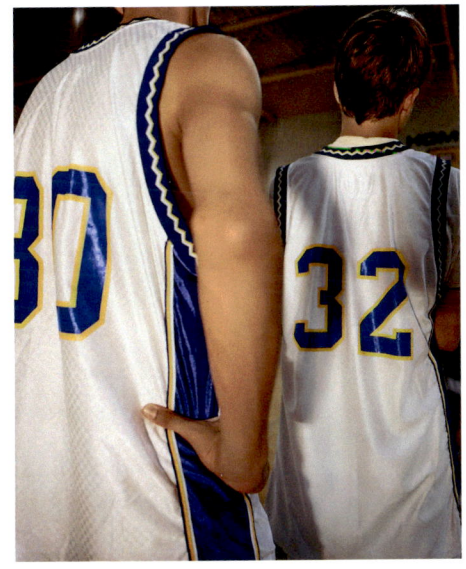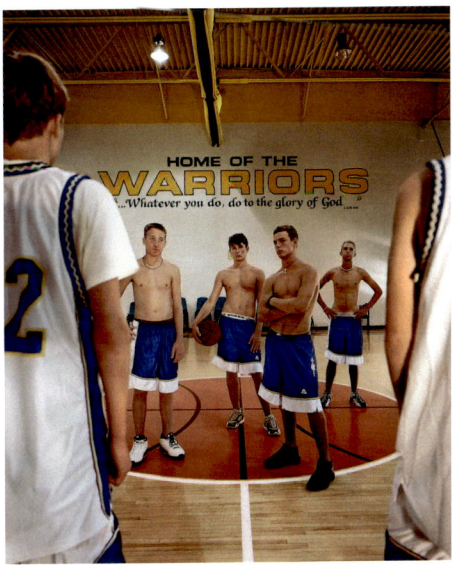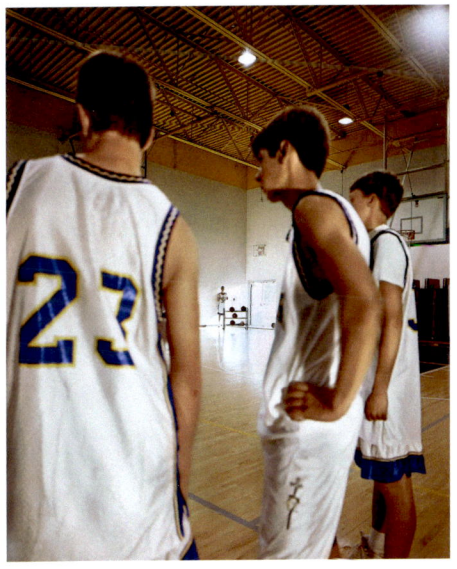

David Huffman

United States, born 1963

In the 1990s, artist David Huffman became interested in scientists' discussions of dark matter, intrigued not only by the research itself but also by the name given to the subject—*dark*, a term often used to describe the unknown. Thinking about the ways in which racism similarly hinges on a lack of understanding, he began weaving together the two ideas. His densely layered paintings read like glimpses into dynamic, distant galaxies of unknowable forms. And yet, careful study reveals the recognizable: surfacing among his expressive brush marks are precisely stenciled graphic motifs of basketballs and the spray-painted negative imprints of both nylon and chain basketball nets—decidedly earthly elements that are often weighted with associations to African American culture.

In sculptural projects, Huffman also turns to the basketball as a cultural symbol and combines its imagery with ideas about space. His pyramids of basketballs evoke the grandeur and power associated with the ritual structures of ancient civilizations. Instead of the heavy stones favored by Egyptian pharaohs or Maya rulers, however, each of his monuments is constructed of 650 rubber basketballs. On one level, the works humorously underscore the almost religious devotion to the sport on the part of so many fans. But there is another, political, aspect to the sculptures. They express the artist's interest in Afrofuturism: the imaging of new worlds through a black perspective. Huffman has noted, "The basketball is a shifting symbol, one that can point to an arena of objectification and exploitation, or toward African American dreams and aspirations that have been realized."[1] In using the ball as an architectural building block, he recognizes both the adversity and success that mark black history, but sees in their sum the potential for monumental triumph.

While structurally the same, each of Huffman's pyramids is composed differently. *Liberation*, his fourth such construction, deliberately uses the colors of the Pan African

> "The basketball is a shifting symbol, one that can point to an arena of objectification and exploitation, or toward African American dreams and aspirations that have been realized."

1. David Huffman, artist's statement, e-mail to the author, February 8, 2019.

Double Jump, 2014
Acrylic, oil, spray paint, printing ink, and glitter on canvas
69 × 69 in.
Courtesy of the artist

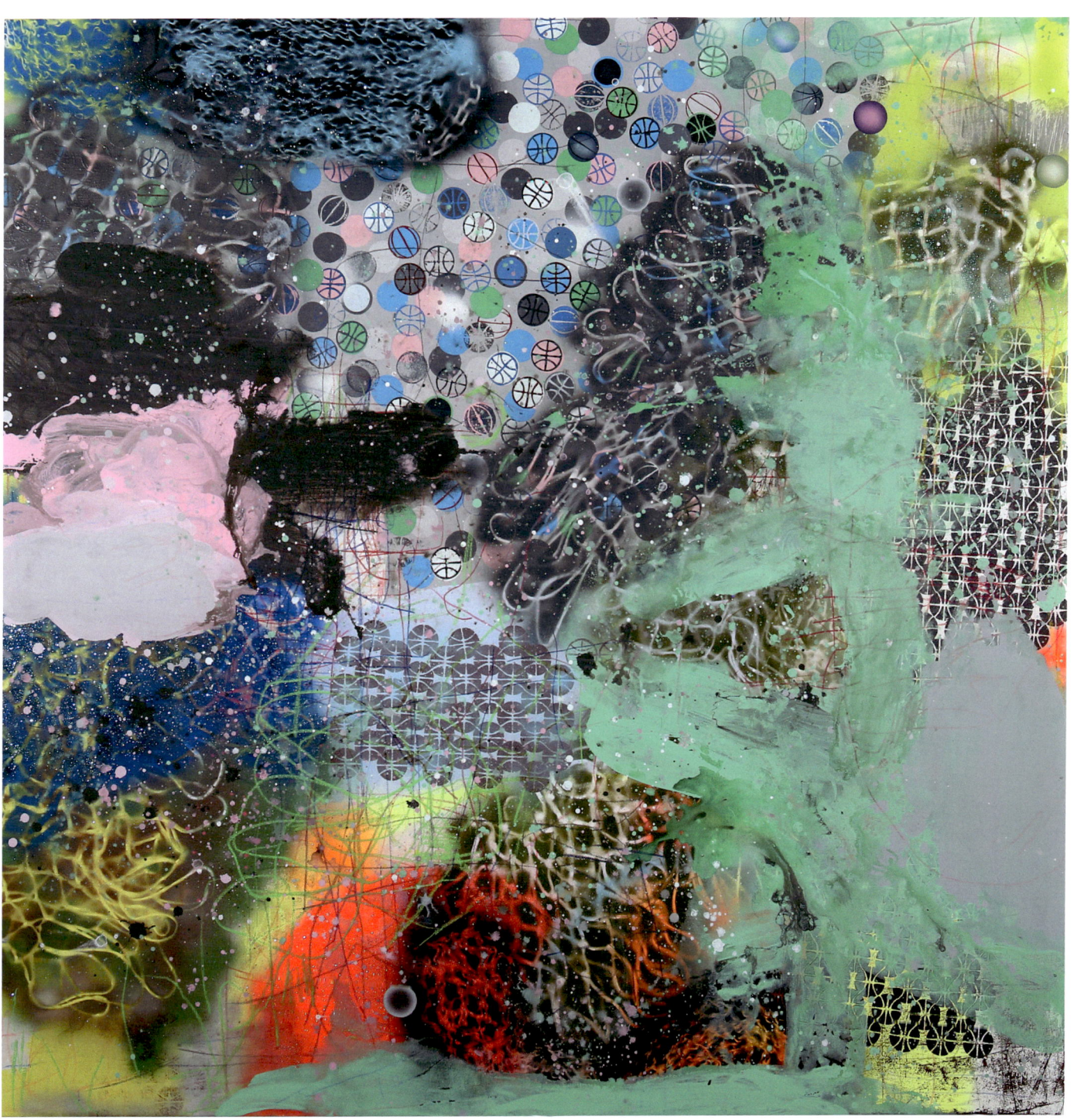

flag. Embedded within the sculpture is an audio track interweaving Dr. Martin Luther King Jr.'s "I Have a Dream" speech with NASA's sonic translation of the electromagnetic waves recorded from Jupiter's largest moon, Ganymede. For *To the Hoop*, Huffman has created his fifth pyramid and a new audio track. He considers all his pyramids to be social sculptures: at the end of each exhibition, the balls are given away to youth sports organizations and charities.

Liberation, 2018
650 rubber basketballs, speakers
and audio track, and painted
wood frame
90 × 120 × 120 in.
Courtesy of the artist

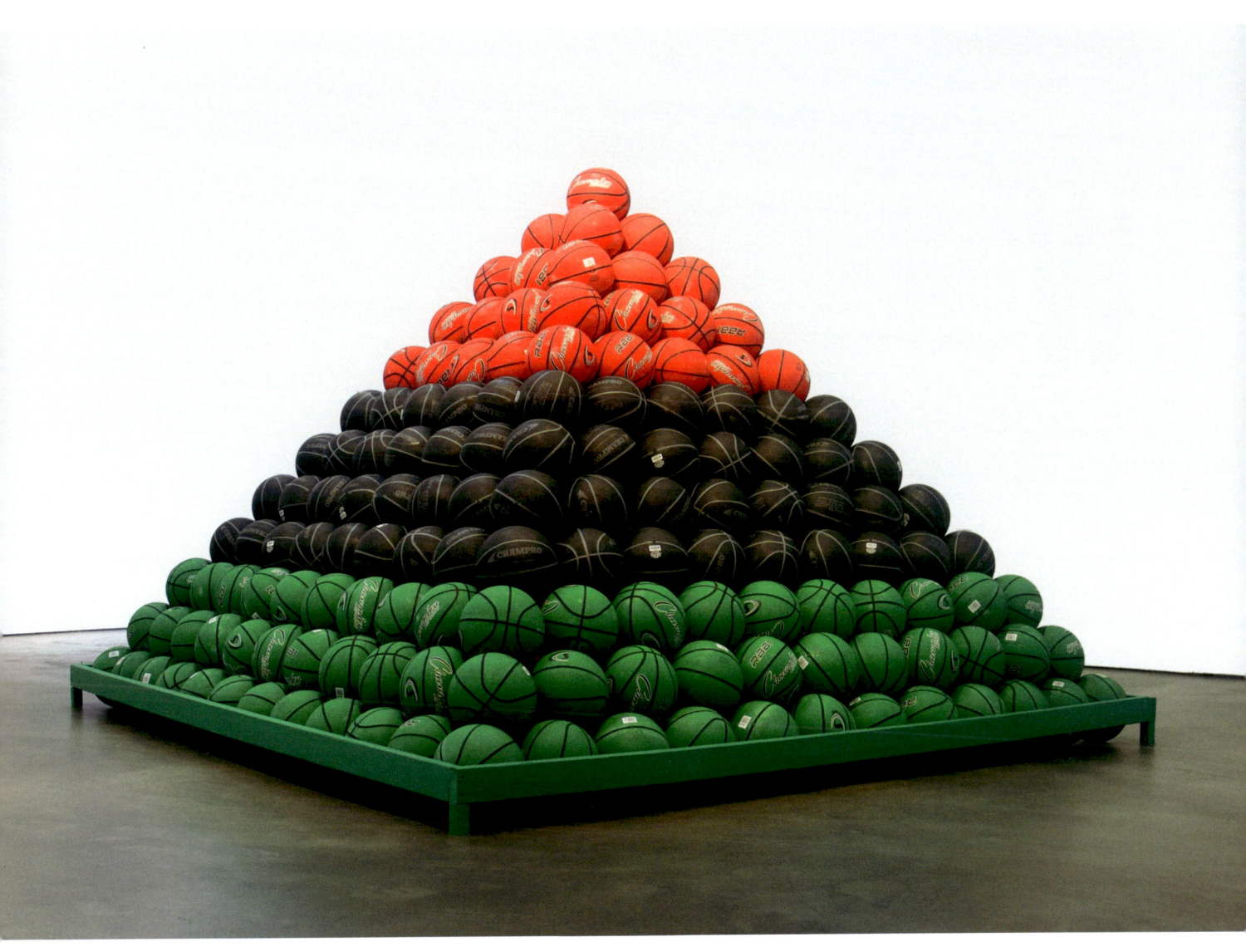

Brian Jungen

Canada, born 1970

With a sharp sense of irony, Brian Jungen creates hybrid artworks that question how we categorize and value objects. A Canadian artist of both European and indigenous heritage, Jungen is interested in art and anthropology—and the dual ways in which we understand objects as both visual and functional. With sly humor, he takes familiar consumer items and deconstructs them, destroying their intended function while reconstructing them into art objects. Frequent among the materials he turns to are those found in basketball paraphernalia, specifically Nike Air Jordan sneakers. Basketball is incredibly popular in many Native communities, and Jungen recalls that when he was a teenager, the shoes were coveted as symbols of status among his peers in the Doig River band of the Dane-zaa First Nation.

In *This Will Not Be Alright*, he has taken the famed shoes apart and sewn them back together. Reassembled on the wall, the objects have become components of a sculpture, their status indeterminate. Although still recognizable as shoes, they also suggest anthropological masks, with the frayed laces appearing as tufts of hair, or an Abstract Expressionist painting with the dangling laces recalling drips of paint. The artwork's title comes from a song by Mary Margaret O'Hara, a singer recognized for her improvisational approach to blending musical styles—a hybrid sensibility not unlike Jungen's own.

This Will Not Be Alright, 2016
Nike Air Jordans
67 × 71 × 14 ½ in.
Courtesy of the artist and
Casey Kaplan Gallery, New York

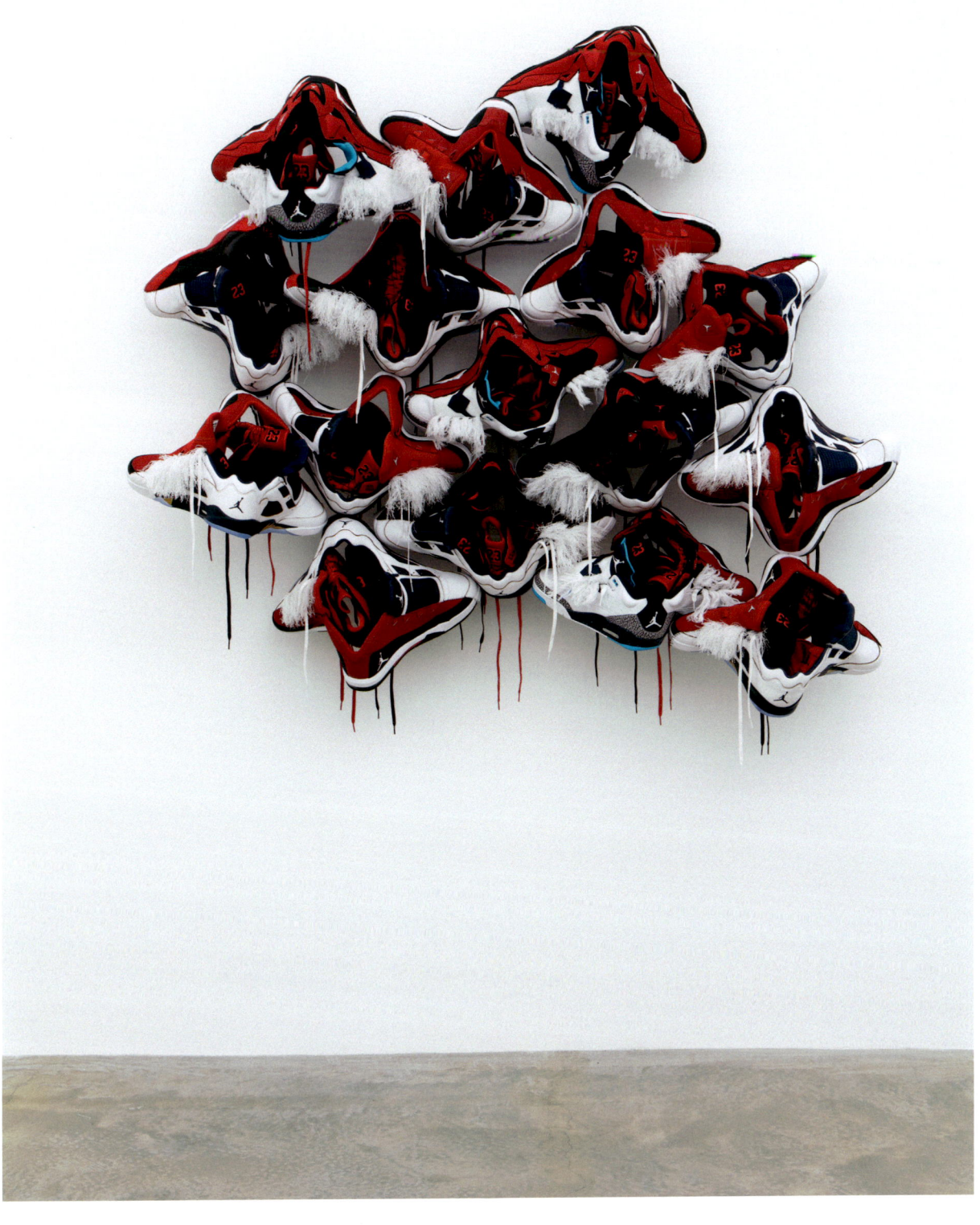

Jeff Koons

United States, born 1955

Jeff Koons's mesmerizing sculpture presents the seemingly impossible: a basketball neither floating nor sinking in a tank of water, hovering in exact balance with its surroundings. Though singular and isolated, it takes on multiple associations. As a golden orb suspended, it evokes the sun. As an object carefully preserved and displayed, it suggests a rare scientific specimen. Koons also philosophically described it as a state of being, "pre-birth."[1] In addition to these natural associations, the ball is loaded with consumer connections: a brand new object unsullied by use and evocative of the hope that superior talent might transport an athlete from humble origins to a life of wealth. When Koons first exhibited the sculpture, he displayed it alongside posters of basketball stars advertising Nike products. He considered those posters to be, like so many advertisements, "great deceivers," offering faulty promises by implicitly saying, "Go for it! I have achieved it. You can achieve it too!"[2]

In the sculpture's title, Koons deliberately specifies the basketball's brand, Spalding, and even its product line, the Dr. J Silver Series. On the ball's surface is the printed replica signature of the famous Philadelphia 76ers player Julius Erving, "Dr. J.," famed for his dunk shot. Dr. J's name brings yet another layer of associations to the work, as the suspended ball recalls the moments of anticipation and uncertainty in the actual game when players and spectators alike watch the ball and player sail through the air to the hoop. That same type of wonder fueled Koons, who has explained that in making this sculpture and others like it, "I really wanted one of these balls to just hover there forever."[3] First made in 1985 with an actual Dr. J Silver Series ball, the sculpture is now exhibited with a replacement replica marked "Dr. JK." Over time, the saline solution in the tank degrades the ball; realizing this, Koons approached Spalding to provide replacement balls. However, the use of Erving's signature was copyrighted, so the company compromised by creating a similar signature using the artist's initials.[4]

1. Jeanne Siegel, "Jeff Koons: Unachievable States of Being," *Arts Magazine* 61, no. 2 (October 1986): 68.
2. Ibid.
3. Norman Rosenthal, *Jeff Koons: Conversations with Norman Rosenthal* (London: Thames & Hudson, 2014), 116.
4. Michael Archer, *Jeff Koons: One Ball Total Equilibrium Tank* (London: Afterall Books, 2011), 89.

One Ball Total Equilibrium Tank (Spalding Dr. J Silver Series),
1985
Glass, steel, sodium chloride reagent, distilled water, and basketball
64 ¾ × 30 ¾ × 13 ¼ in.
Edition
Art Bridges, Bentonville, Arkansas

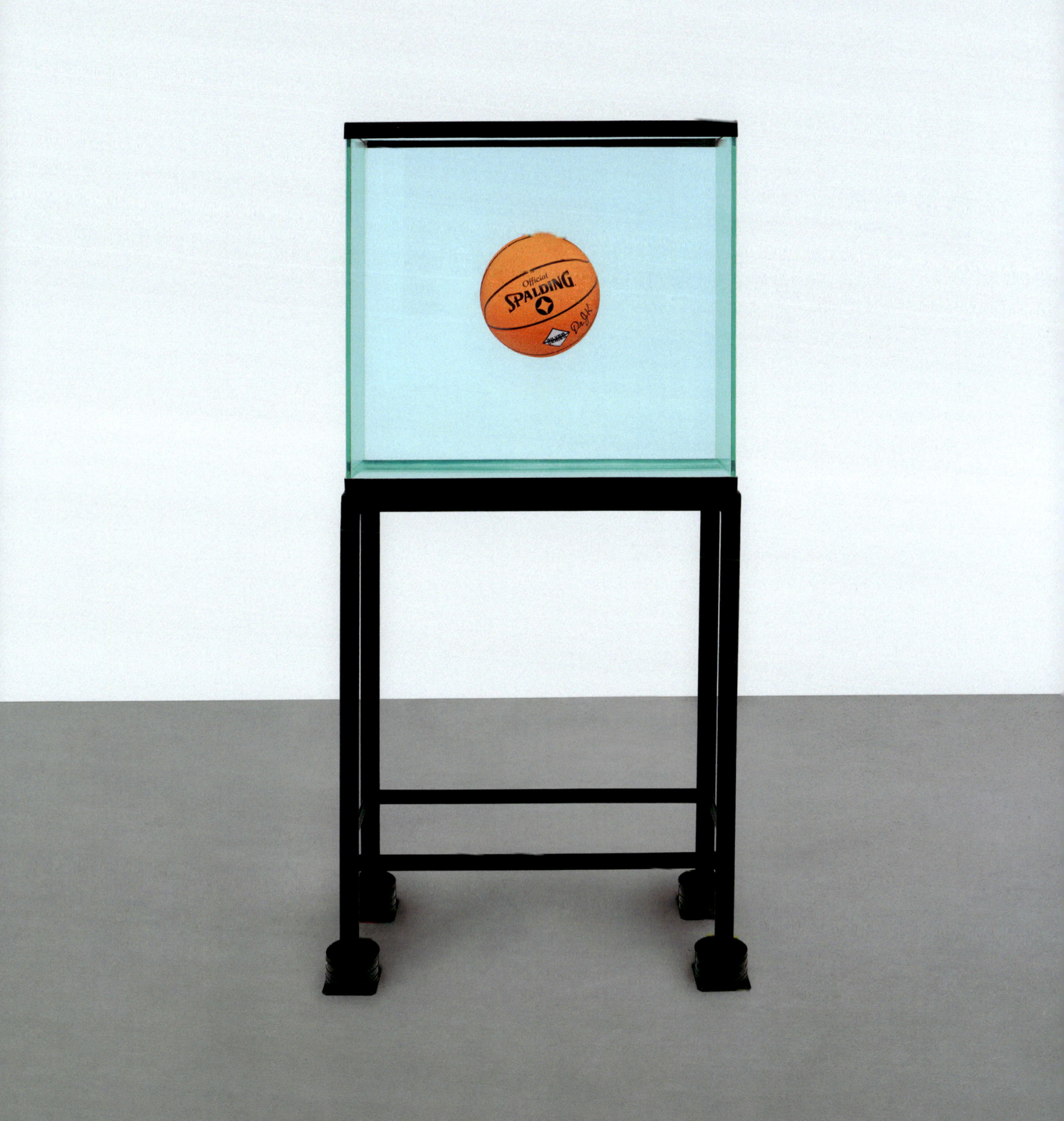

Suzanne McClelland

United States, born 1959

B y 2004, less than a decade old, the Women's National Basketball Association had expanded from its original eight teams to thirteen, and more than ten million fans had attended its games. Despite this success, when Suzanne McClelland went looking for WNBA team jerseys at the NBA store on New York's Fifth Avenue, she recalls, "The women's jerseys were relegated to one messy circular display rack near the bathrooms in the basement . . . greatly reduced in price."[1] In *Well Hung*, with its sly, double-entendre title, she gives the garments a far more triumphant display. Adorned with ribbons and hair bows, embellished with pearls and sequins, and punctuated with feathery pom-poms, her collection of jerseys hangs on the wall like a vibrant patchwork quilt or raucous celebration banner.

The festive tone stands in stark contrast to the circumstances in which McClelland made the work. In the wake of the 2003 Iraq War, the ongoing context of the war in Afghanistan, and President George W. Bush's reelection campaign, McClelland was thinking about coalitions and taking sides. Specifically, she considered the term *draft*, in the context of both the military and sports. When soldiers are drafted, their recruitment is compulsory, but they know they will be fighting for their country. When sports players are drafted, their service is voluntary, but they do not know for which team they will play. In both instances, strangers don a uniform to indicate their collective identity. That unity might be mentally and emotionally tenuous as fellow recruits work to bond; it might also be literally transitory as soldiers are sent to new assignments or players traded to other teams. In light of such thoughts of instability, McClelland determined not to sew the jerseys together, but affix them with safety pins and bows, giving as much attention to each flexible seam as to each individual jersey. Further emphasizing its provisional nature, she packs the artwork for transport in a WNBA duffle bag.

1. Suzanne McClelland, e-mail to the author, June 11, 2018.

Well Hung, 2004
WNBA jerseys, silk, plastic pearls, sequins, ribbon, fake fur, feather trim, rope, and WNBA duffle bag
Dimensions variable, approximately 8 × 12 ft.
Courtesy of the artist and Shane Campbell Gallery, Chicago

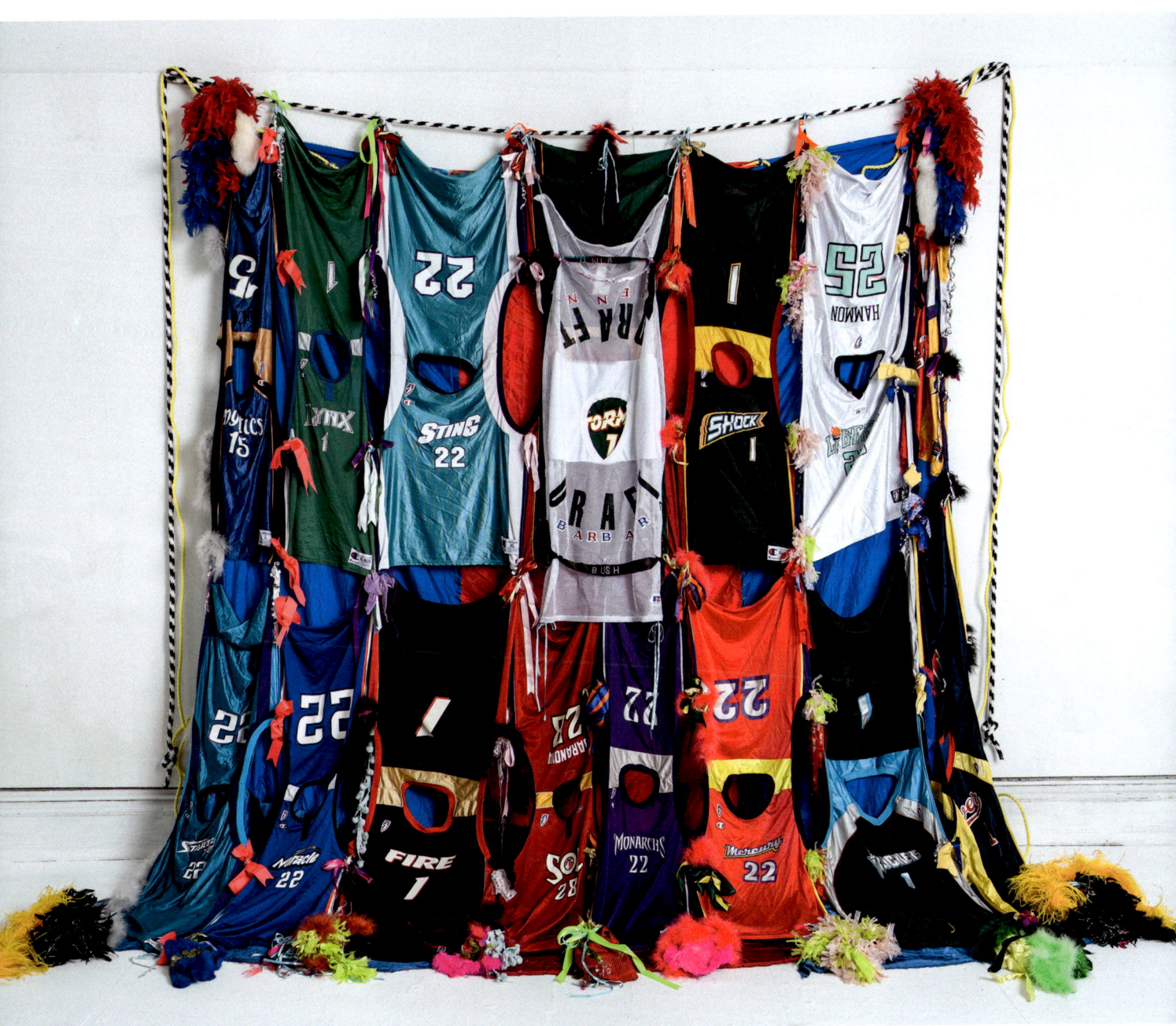

Esmaa Mohamoud

Canada, born 1992

Esmaa Mohamoud grew up as the only daughter in a family of five children, raised by immigrant parents with traditional views regarding gender roles. Her mother would insist she put on a dress before going out to play, but Mohamoud would top the dress with her beloved Vince Carter Toronto Raptors basketball jersey. Her mother would then admonish, "You are not one of the boys." That comment inspired the title of the artist's recent body of photographs, in which she probes gender roles and stereotypes by posing men and women in basketball jerseys that have been transformed into corseted ball gowns. In these two images, the models are shot from behind with their heads bowed such that their identities remain anonymous. In contrast to the energy associated with the game, they register a decided stillness, one that can be read as defiant or contemplative.

As much as Mohamoud is interested in asserting women's voices and gender equity from a female perspective, she is equally concerned with the ways in which men are pressured to accept rigid definitions of what it means to be male. She notes that it was incredibly difficult to find a male model who was willing to wear one of the dresses—even just to pose for an art project—for fear that doing so would threaten his masculinity.

One of the Boys (Red Back), 2017
Color inkjet print
60 × 40 in.
Edition
Courtesy of the artist and
Georgia Scherman Projects, Toronto

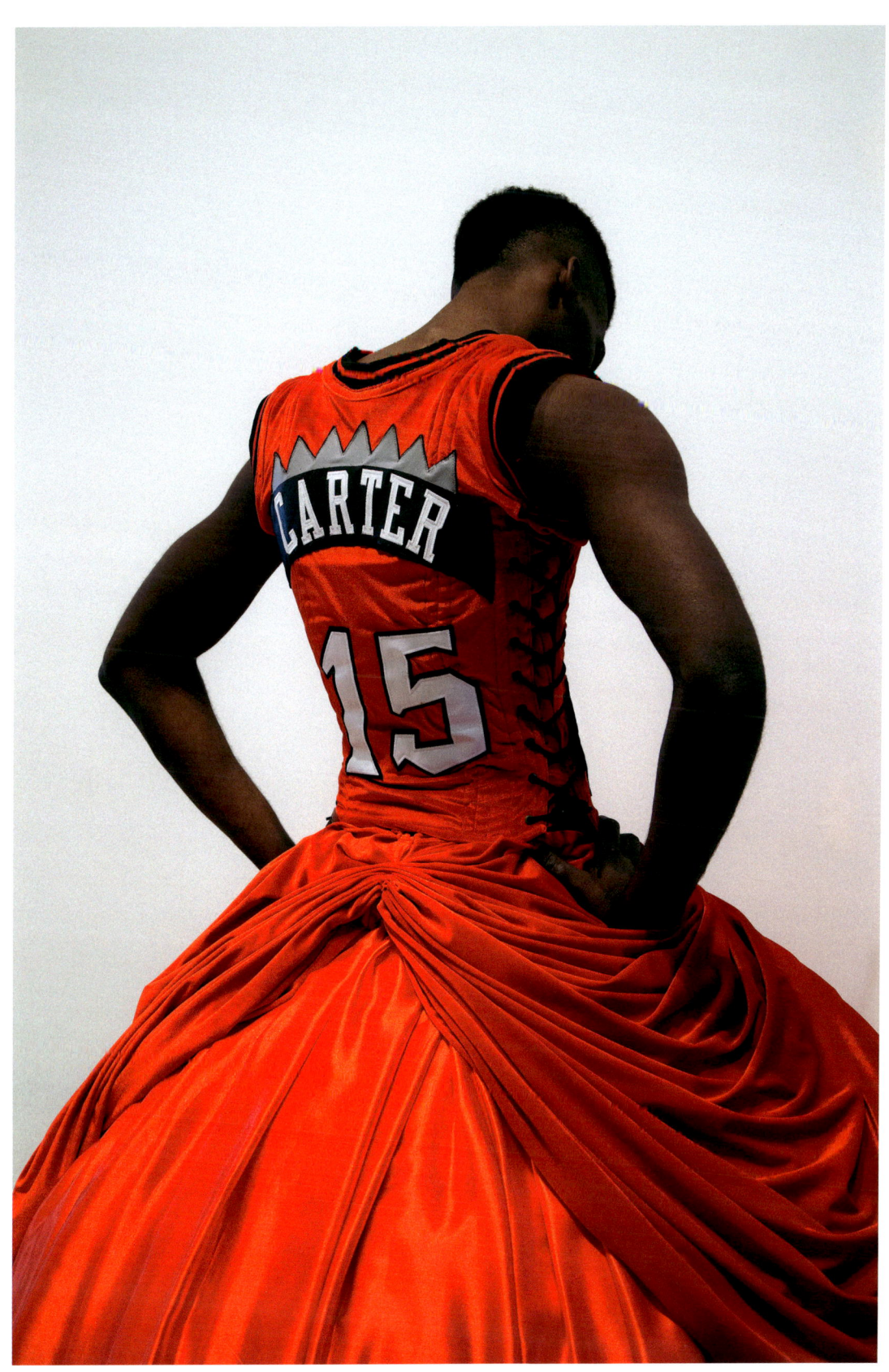

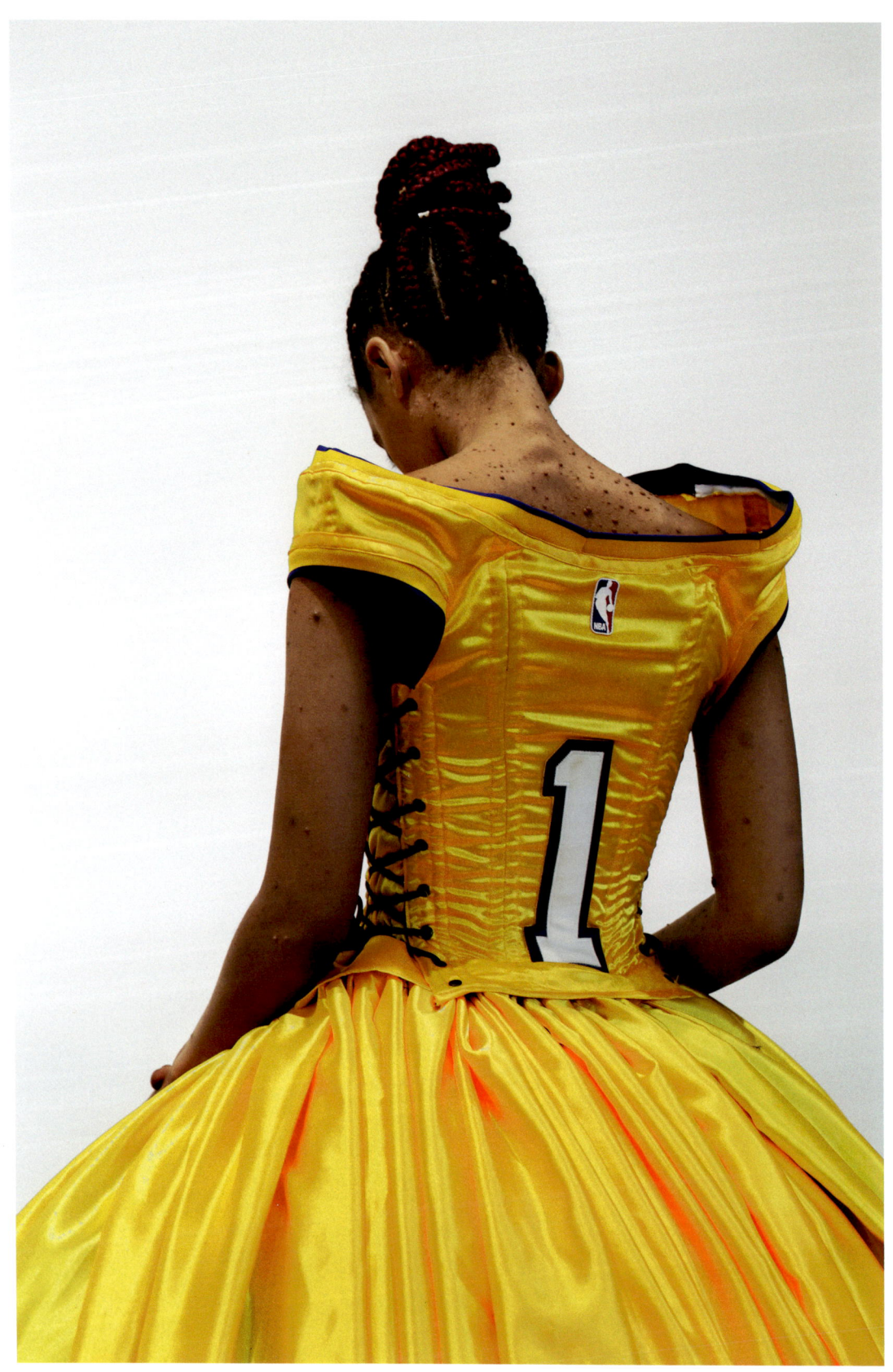

One of the Boys (Yellow Back), 2018
Color inkjet print
60 × 40 in.
Edition
Courtesy of the artist and
Georgia Scherman Projects, Toronto

Maria Molteni

United States, born 1983

with New Craft Artists in Action (NCAA)

Various artists, established 2010

Maria Molteni works at the intersections of craft, activism, and athletics. In 2010 she founded New Craft Artists in Action (NCAA), a collective that works on the participatory project *Net Works*. The group invites individuals to help them knit and crochet nets for bare hoops found on public basketball courts in overlooked and underused spaces. NCAA gives the hoops—and the courts—a colorful life in the hope of building "proactive, inclusive relationships between artists, athletes, and neighbors."[1]

The project stems from Molteni's therapeutic practice of shooting free throws when stuck or frustrated in the studio. One day, she realized that the hoop she was using had no net. She had long been interested in the traditions of handmaking and gift giving, and she realized that a net was something she could both make and give to the neighborhood. By expanding the project and inviting others to join, Molteni celebrates the game's ability to bring people together, offer a form of recreation, and provide an outlet for personal expression. Molteni offers the festive hoops to any and all who wish to enjoy them—regardless of wealth, skill, or status. She and her collaborators "hope to empower team players who have been warming the bench for too long." They have published an illustrated book of instructions for how to make nets, thus encouraging others to expand the project.

In addition to *Net Works*, Molteni and her collaborators also make elaborate basketball court murals and create immersive gallery installations of handmade nets, bunting, banners, and other elements. Brightly colored and playful, they resonate with the same festive aura that characterizes the public works. Molteni and NCAA have created a new net installation specifically for *To the Hoop*.

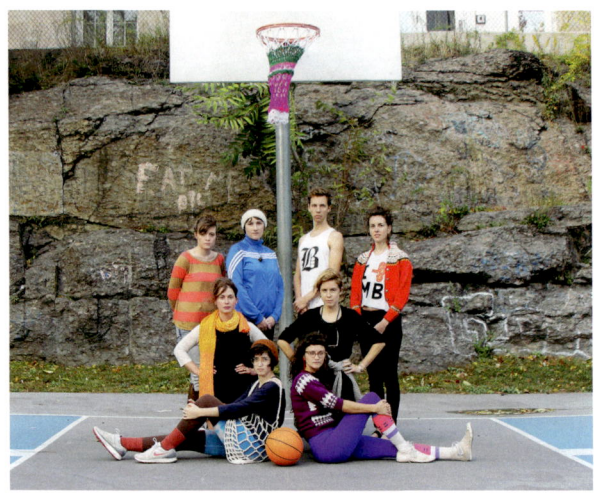

Team photo with some of the Boston-based
NCAA collaborators, 2012

1. NCAA, "Warm Up," in *Net Works: Learn to Craft Handmade Nets for Empty Basketball Hoops in Your Neighborhood*, ed. Maria Molteni (Self Published, 2014), 8.

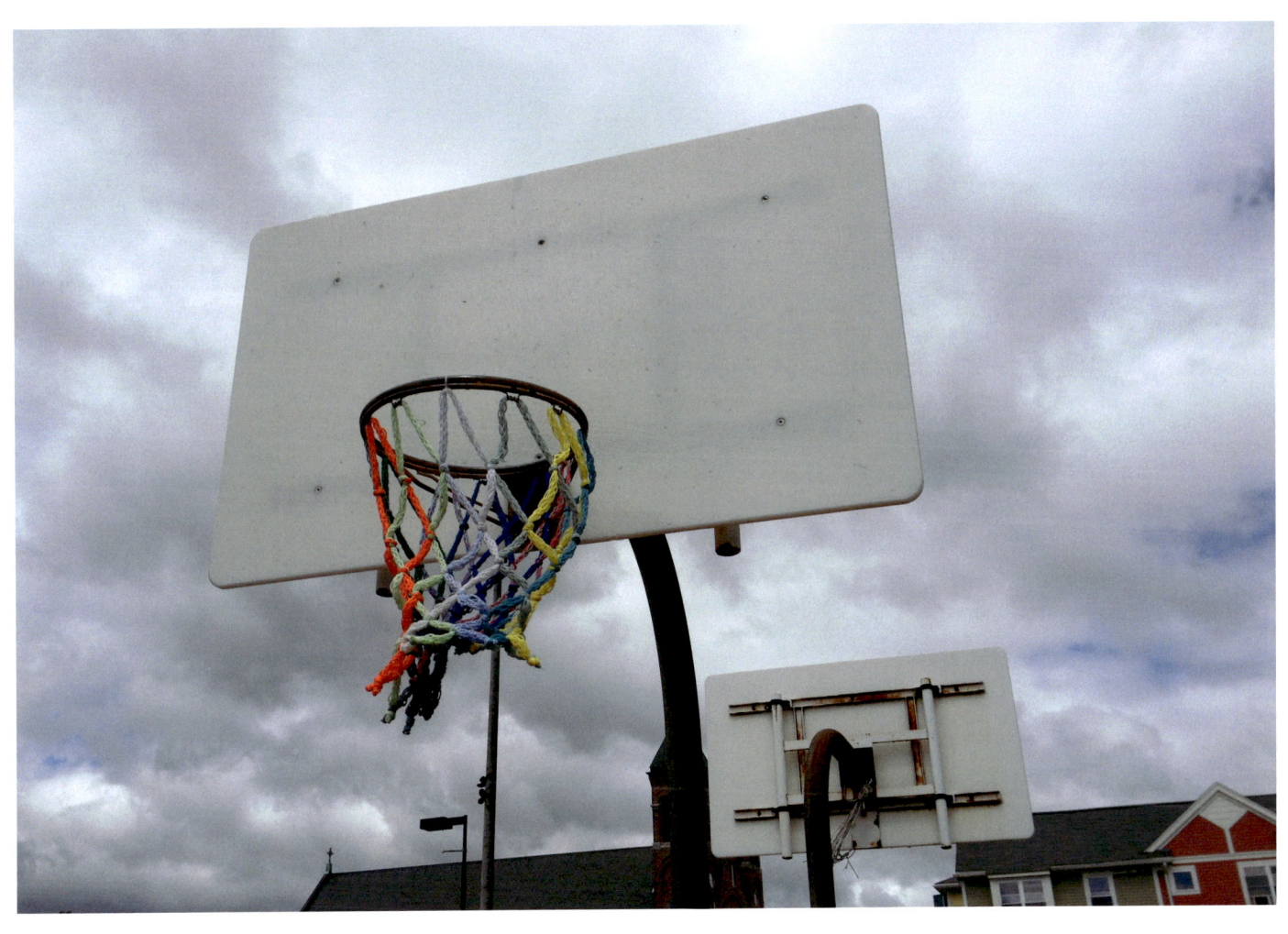

Cushing House Net Work, 2014
From the project *Net Works*, 2010–ongoing
Handmade nylon yarn net installed on
community hoop, D Street, South Boston
Approximately 4 ½ × 6 × 1 ½ ft.
Courtesy of the artist and NCAA

Paul Pfeiffer

United States, born 1966

Paul Pfeiffer's deceptively realistic photographs of basketball moments are visually akin to spiritual revelations. Pfeiffer searches out images found in the online archives of the NBA and digitally removes contextual details large and small—players on the court, coaches on the sidelines, jersey colors and numbers, advertisements on stadium billboards. He creates his uncanny images through this reductive process of erasure until seemingly straightforward scenes are as mysterious for what is absent as for what they record. In the first of the pictures here, the spectacular focal point is a single airborne player frozen as he reaches upward in a dramatic twist. The elongated figure bisects the composition from top to bottom. Glowing light seems to radiate from his fingertips, bathing his outstretched arm and heightening the gesture's drama.

Light is similarly the key element in the second image. A camera's flash creates a brilliant orb that hovers in the middleground. In the foreground, a woman and child face the glow with arms outstretched—a secular Virgin and Child in rapture. Just above the child's head, the cruciform feature of the shot clock subtly underscores the religious symbolism. Moreover, Pfeiffer explicitly gave this series a religious title *Four Horsemen of the Apocalypse*, after artist Albrecht Dürer's famous fifteenth-century illustration of the Book of Revelation. Pfeiffer is interested in the ways in which certain visual tropes persist through time, especially the gestures and compositions that we read as dramatic and spectacular. "I tend to imagine the continuities between something as old as painting and something as new as a live broadcast of a basketball game. The way a basketball game is shot owes a lot to painting."[1] In his reappropriated and altered photographs, Pfeiffer both underscores that connection and emphasizes the epic, even religious, stature often accorded to sporting events.

1. Paul Pfeiffer, in "Paul Pfeiffer," by Jennifer Gonzalez, *BOMB*, April, 2003, accessed online March 1, 2019.

> "I tend to imagine the continuities between something as old as painting and something as new as a live broadcast of a basketball game. The way a basketball game is shot owes a lot to painting."

Four Horsemen of the Apocalypse (18), 2004
Fujiflex digital C-print
48 × 60 in.
Courtesy of the artist and
Paula Cooper Gallery, New York

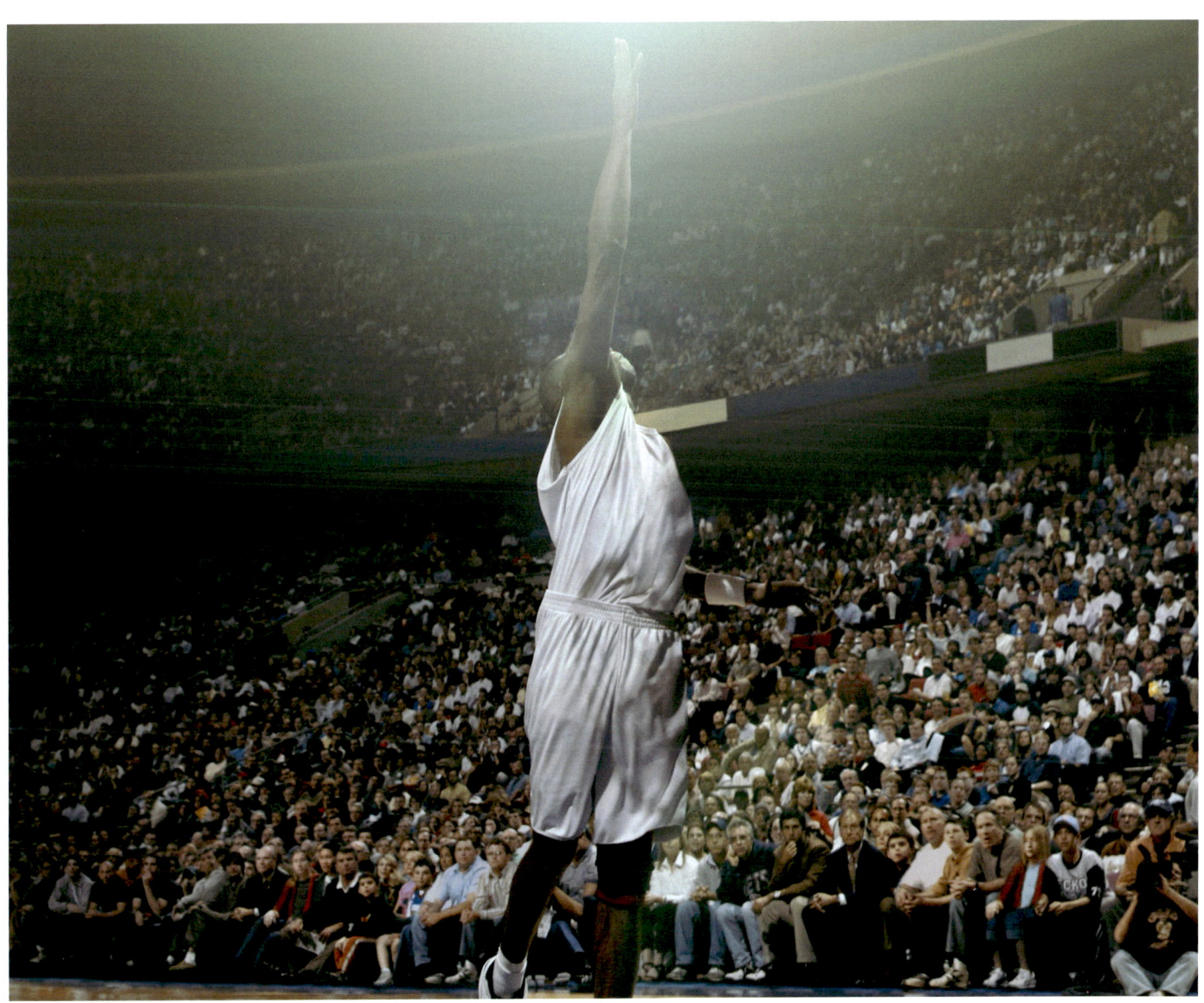

Four Horsemen of the
Apocalypse (25), 2006
Fujiflex digital C-print
48 × 63 ½ in.
Courtesy of the artist and
Paula Cooper Gallery, New York

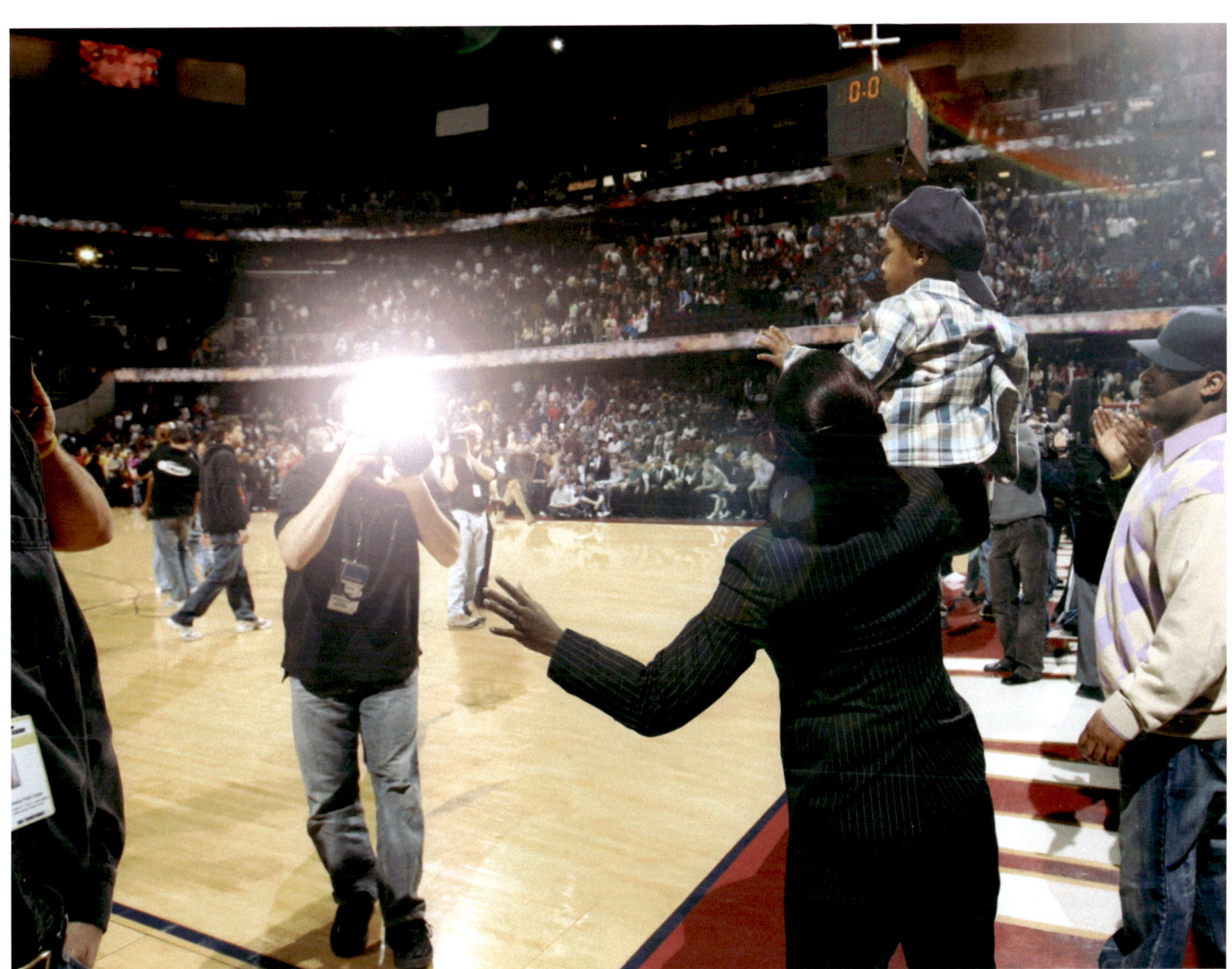

Joyce J. Scott

United States, born 1948

J oyce J. Scott's sculptures pointedly refuse contemporary art-world hierarchies. Crafted largely of intricate beadwork, they at once honor her African American heritage and culture, draw from a global span of craft traditions, and reference spiritual practices of different religions. In this sculpture, Buddha sits in his iconic cross-legged lotus pose, surrounded by enigmatic symbols. Instead of a traditional halo of light framing his face, a ladder loops around his head—a reference to Jacob's heaven-bound steps in the Judeo-Christian Book of Genesis, which is frequently invoked in African American spirituals of mobility and liberation. Among the ladder's upper loops, one finds a golden figure emerging from the Buddha's head; it recalls the cranial bump that traditionally indicates his wisdom, but it takes human form and reads as a basketball player raising a ball upward.

At the ladder's base, a figurative silhouette spills from a bowl and lies flush against the ground. Scott describes this flattened form as a "submissive player," one that has forgone the ladder of success for a more modest, spiritual path.[1] Traditionally revered for teaching a course of balance known as the Middle Way, Buddha here sits in the space between ambition and humility. Scott's title for the sculpture, *Buddha Gives Basketball to the Ghetto*, adds another interpretive dimension—comically framing Buddha not only as a spiritual leader but also as the source of basketball's popularity in poor urban locales. Given notions of basketball as means to move from poverty to wealth, Scott's Buddha suggests that players might want to not only dream of potential financial rewards, but also consider the philosophical dividends they can reap from the game.

1. Joyce J. Scott e-mail to the author, April 29, 2018.

*Buddha Gives Basketball
to the Ghetto*, 1991
Glass and plastic beads,
wire, and thread
18 × 15 × 14 in.
Collection of Carol Cole Levin

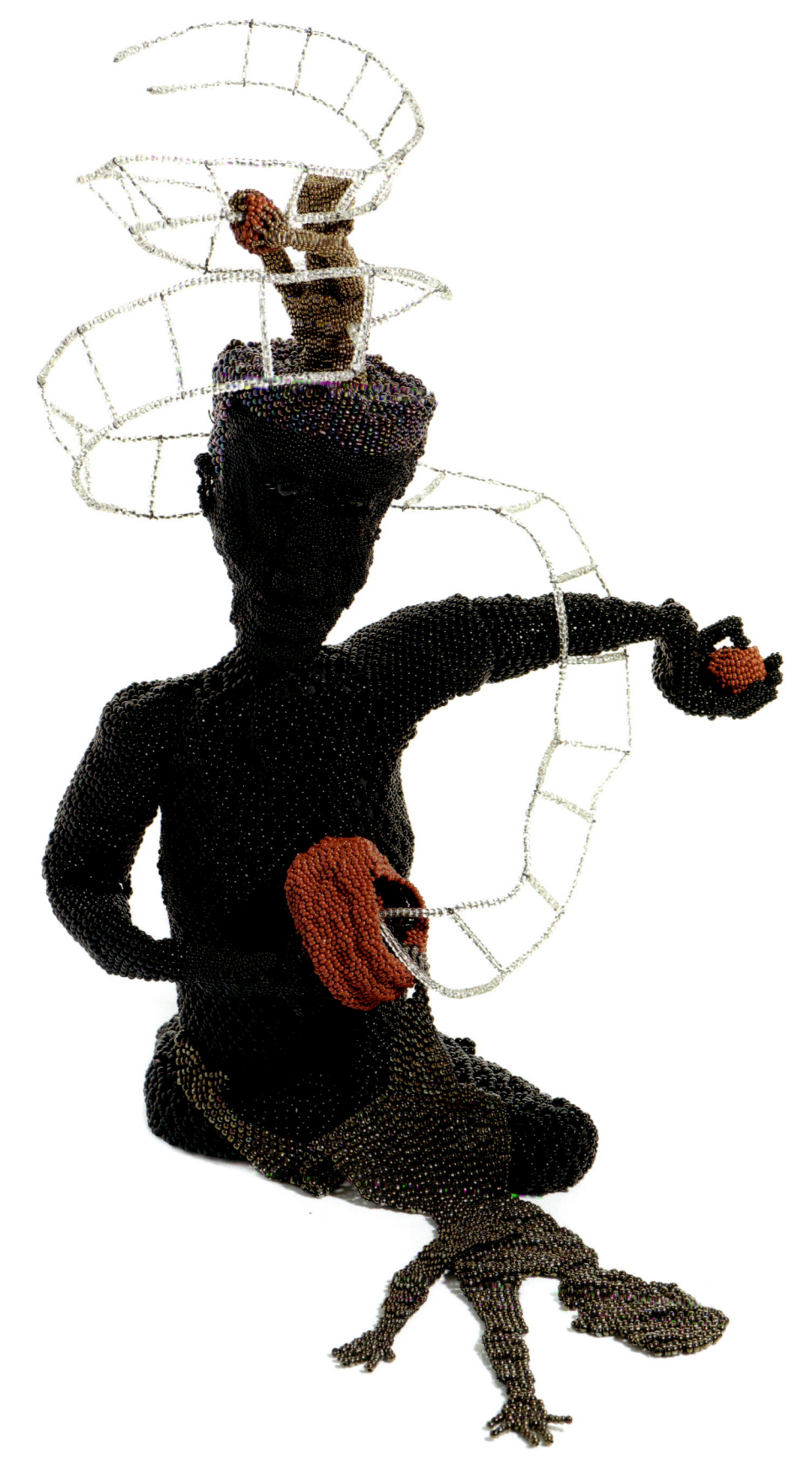

Lorna Simpson

United States, born 1960

Lorna Simpson's *Poets* comprises two sets of images arranged in a loose grid. On the left are nineteen silver rectangles, each marked with one or more black circles. Differently sized and placed, the floating dots suggest a hidden logic or code. On the right side of the installation, that meaning is revealed: in reproductions of newspaper photographs of mid-twentieth-century basketball players, each dot marks the location of the basketball they hold. Working by hand, Simpson emphasized the photographs' original crop marks, overlaying each editorial notation with acrylic and oil stick. In doing so, she reminds us that images—like identities and histories—are never to be taken at face value; deliberate decisions and specific contexts shape what we know.

Mounted on the wall, some images are hung upright, others turned sideways. The seemingly improvisational placements underscore both the fast pace of the game's players and the quick mark-making of the editors. Simpson's title, *Poets*, not only acknowledges the distinctive styles of both the athletes and the image makers; it refers specifically to the storied basketball teams of Baltimore's Paul Laurence Dunbar High School, named for the esteemed African American author. The school produced some of the nation's best student teams, especially during the 1950s. That moment, of course, was also marked by the desegregation of schools and the growing civil rights movement. More than a half-century later, Simpson's complex arrangement of obscured and "uncovered" photographs underscores the deep connections between the histories of basketball and race relations in the United States.

Poets, 2013
19 framed black-and-white photographs with acrylic and oil stick; 19 aluminum boxes with acrylic
Dimensions variable
Courtesy of the artist and Hauser & Wirth

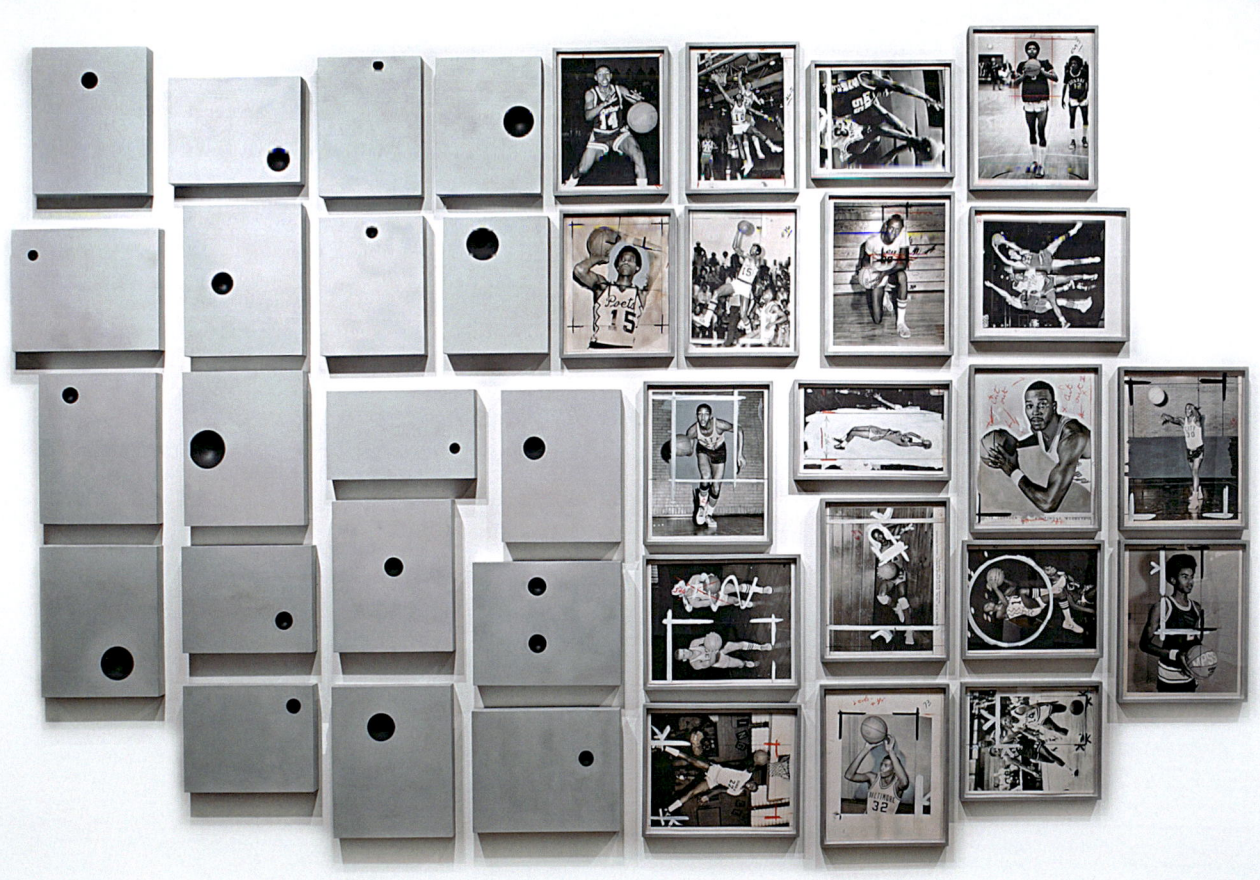

Victor Solomon

United States, born 1981

Using stained glass, gold leaf, crystal, and other opulent materials, Victor Solomon creates basketball backboards and hoops inspired by the décor of palaces and cathedrals. The homage is both sincere and sarcastic. Recalling his youth as a mixed-race kid in East Boston, he remembers that it was on the basketball courts of his neighborhood that racial and ethnic distinctions disappeared; the game created a space in which participation was predicated on skill rather than skin color or family background. At the same time as his sculptures celebrate that inclusivity, they also acknowledge profound economic divides between the many who aspire to become basketball stars and the few who achieve that wealthy status. The precariousness of that fame is likewise a part of the work: while designed to precisely mimic actual backboards and hoops, their fragile beauty renders Solomon's versions useless, unable to withstand the shock of a ball hitting them.

Church is the first instance in which Solomon has mounted a backboard on an actual stanchion rather than on the wall. Pulled out into the space of the gallery, it can be lit from behind, further emphasizing its references to the stained-glass windows of Christian sanctuaries—as called out in the sculpture's title. Such a spiritual association aligns with popular language in which sports fans are described as "devoted" to their teams or humorously refer to sports as their "religion." That phrasing can be tongue-in-cheek, but Solomon's exquisite and meticulously crafted Church appears more earnest than lighthearted, an acknowledgment that for many basketball can provide a sense of community and even refuge from daily struggles, comforts akin to those one might also find in a house of worship.

Church, 2019
Stained glass, 24k-gold-plated
hand-wrought steel, acrylic,
and crystals
10 × 4 × 4 ft.
Courtesy of the artist

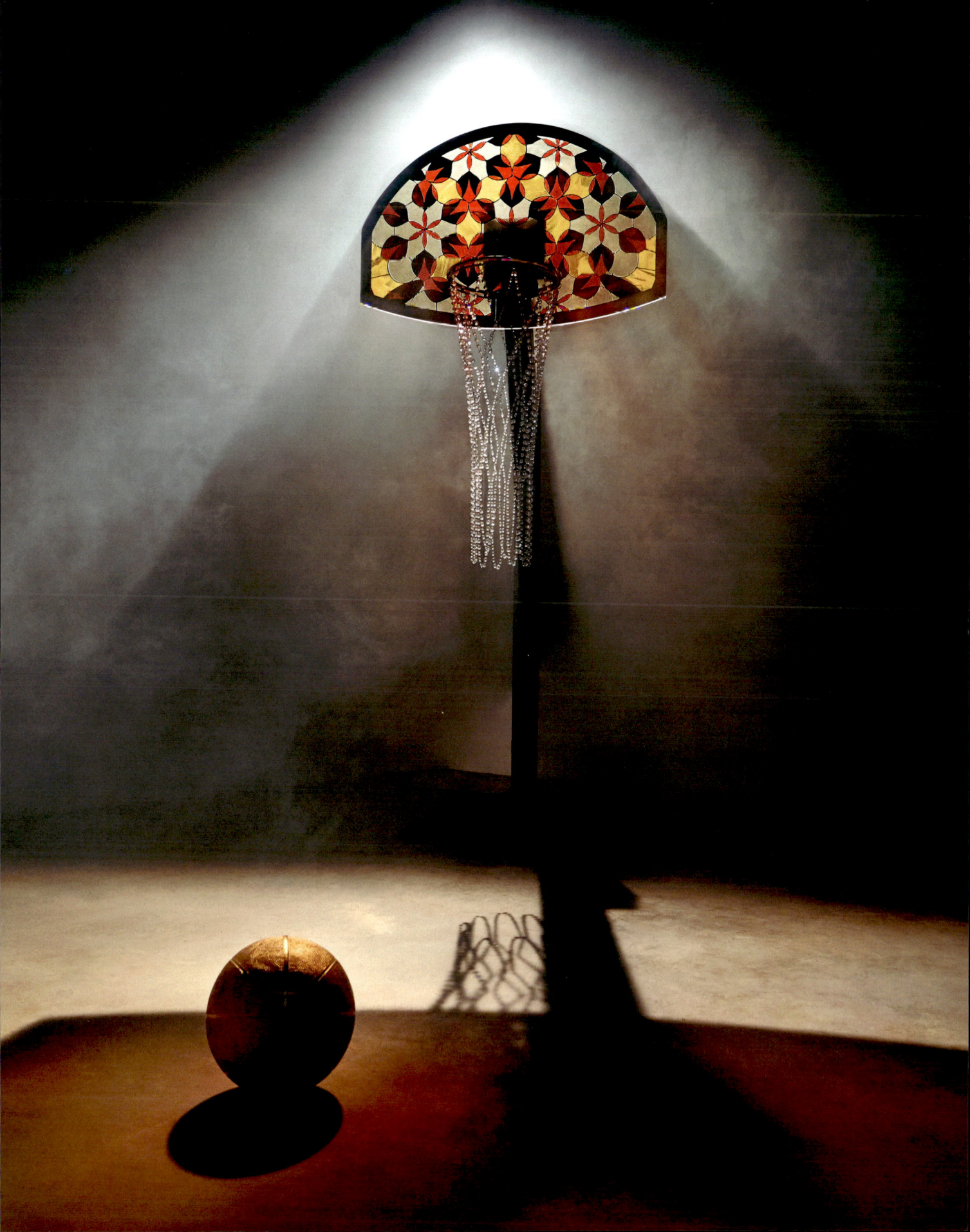

Hank Willis Thomas

United States, born 1976

I n his multimedia work, Hank Willis Thomas explores the intersections of race and commerce by recontextual- izing advertisements, logos, and other mass-produced corporate imagery. Frequent among the pictures he deploys is the iconic Michael Jordan "Jumpman" sil- houette used to brand Nike apparel. With biting humor, Thomas plays with the Air Jordan sneaker logo as a symbol for success, power, and fame—reimagining it with a third leg as a way to suggest the impossibility of its promises. The athletic talent and resulting success of a player like Jordan are unspeakably rare; the vast majority will never soar to that level but instead need sturdier footing. Additionally, the extra leg recalls the urban slang for a penis, thus also mocking the ways in which popular sports culture rein- forces notions of hypermasculinity.

As a student of history, Thomas's consideration of brand- ing extends through time. Describing *Branded Head*, he states, "I started thinking about how slaves were branded as a sign of ownership and how today so many of us brand ourselves and increasingly live in a branded society."[1] He is particularly concerned about the commodification and branding of black bodies, especially those of male ath- letes: "For so many African American men especially, the idea of ascending is chained to ascending through sports and entertainment."[2] Such ideas take poignant form in his photograph of a black man in profile. Cropped so that the features of his face are missing, the figure becomes anon- ymous. Marked only by the Nike swoosh formed of scar tissue on the side of his head, he is transformed from an individual to a thing, no longer a subject but an object.

"For so many African American men especially, the idea of ascending is chained to ascending through sports and entertainment."

1. Hank Willis Thomas, "What Goes Without Saying," in Celeste-Marie Bernier and Hannah Durkin, eds., *Visualizing Slavery* (Liverpool: Liverpool University Press: 2016), 39.
2. Ibid.

Something to Stand On: The Third Leg, 2007
MDF with polyurethane coat
36 × 30 in.
Courtesy of the artist and
Jack Shainman Gallery, New York

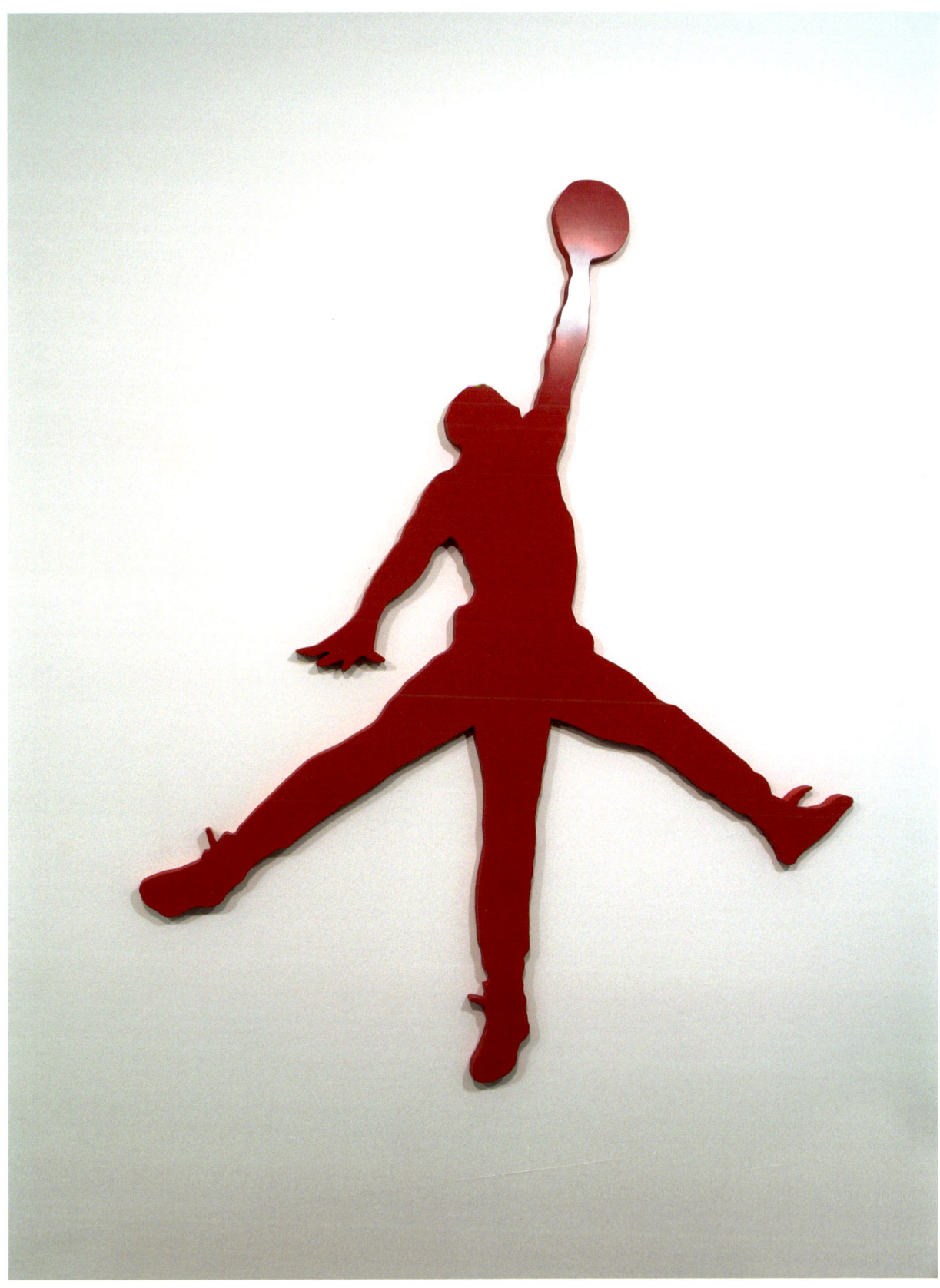

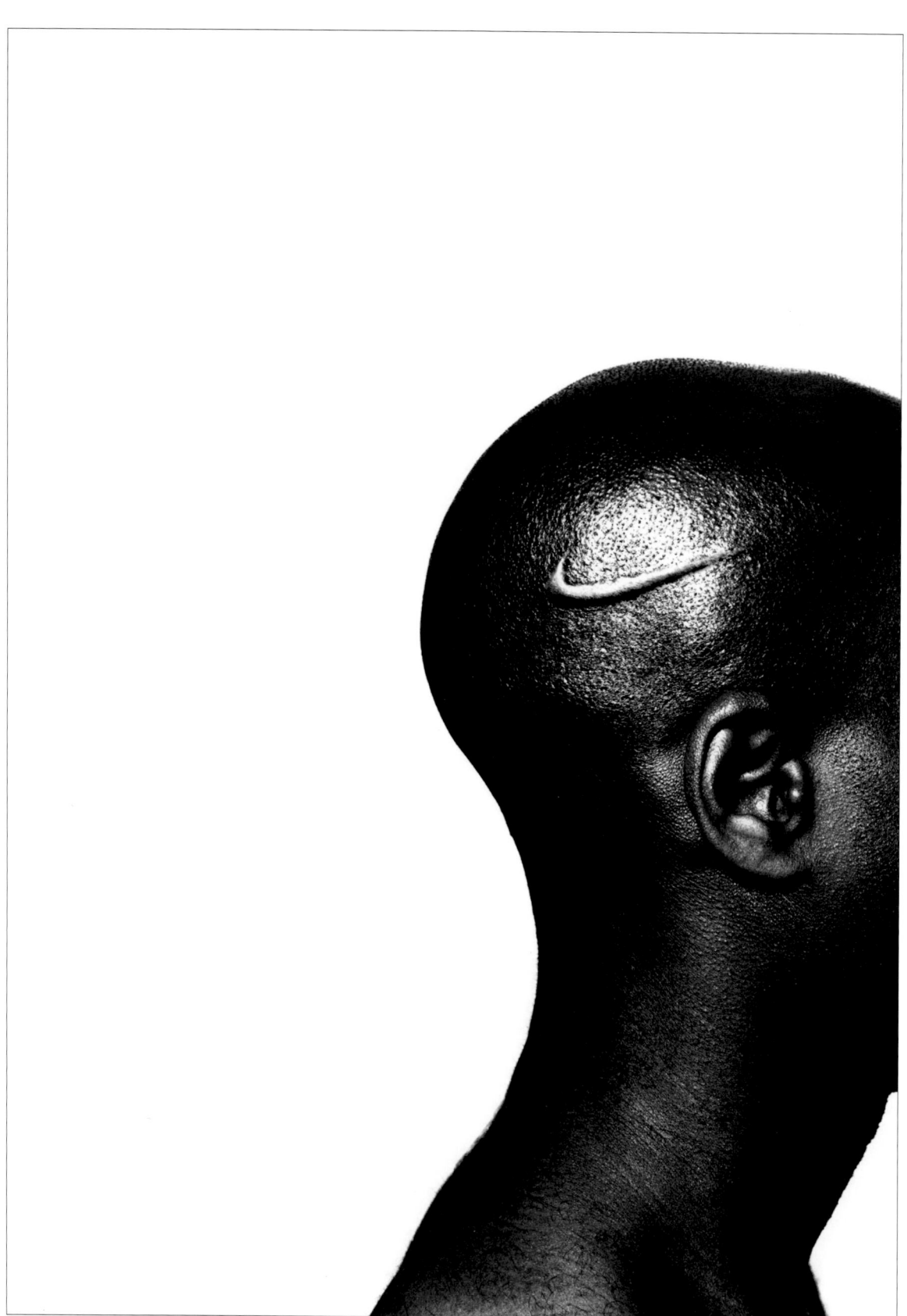

Branded Head, 2003
Lambda photograph
30 × 20 in.
Edition
Courtesy of the artist and
Jack Shainman Gallery, New York

Nari Ward

United States, born Jamaica, 1963

Nari Ward creates sculptures with rich, evocative surfaces made from discarded materials that he finds and accumulates. For *Album*, Ward overlaid a round form with basketball trading cards inked to leave only the balls in each image exposed. Scattered across the dark surface, these bright orange dots flicker like a crowded galaxy of stars—truly an apt metaphor. Ward has turned to the image of the night sky in a number of works. He recalls his amazement learning in a high school science class that "by the time the light has gotten to us, those stars no longer exist."[1] In *Album*, star players whose pictures were coveted and traded have become a span of darkness lit by the emblem of the game they played.

Embossed repeatedly around the rim of the sculpture is the word *bebop*, a term for a fast, improvisational type of jazz paced much like the game of basketball. The non-stop repetition of the word around the form's circumference implies movement—the revolution of a spinning record or a basketball in play. The overall circular shape echoes those of the basketballs dotting its surface, and, along with its black hue, evoke a vinyl record, perhaps playing a bebop classic. More so than any other contemporary sport, basketball is culturally affiliated with music, specifically hip hop, which is often described in relationship to jazz. Ward connects these associations along with the dots, so to speak, a stargazer mindful of the culture and the court.

Album, 2011
Stencil ink, basketball trading cards, glue, and aluminum
50 × 50 in.
Nasher Museum of Art, Duke University, Durham, North Carolina, Museum Purchase with funds provided by Marjorie and Michael Levine, 2011.16.1

1. Nari Ward, "A Segue into History," produced by the Vilcek Foundation, February 14, 2017; accessed on YouTube, March 6, 2019.

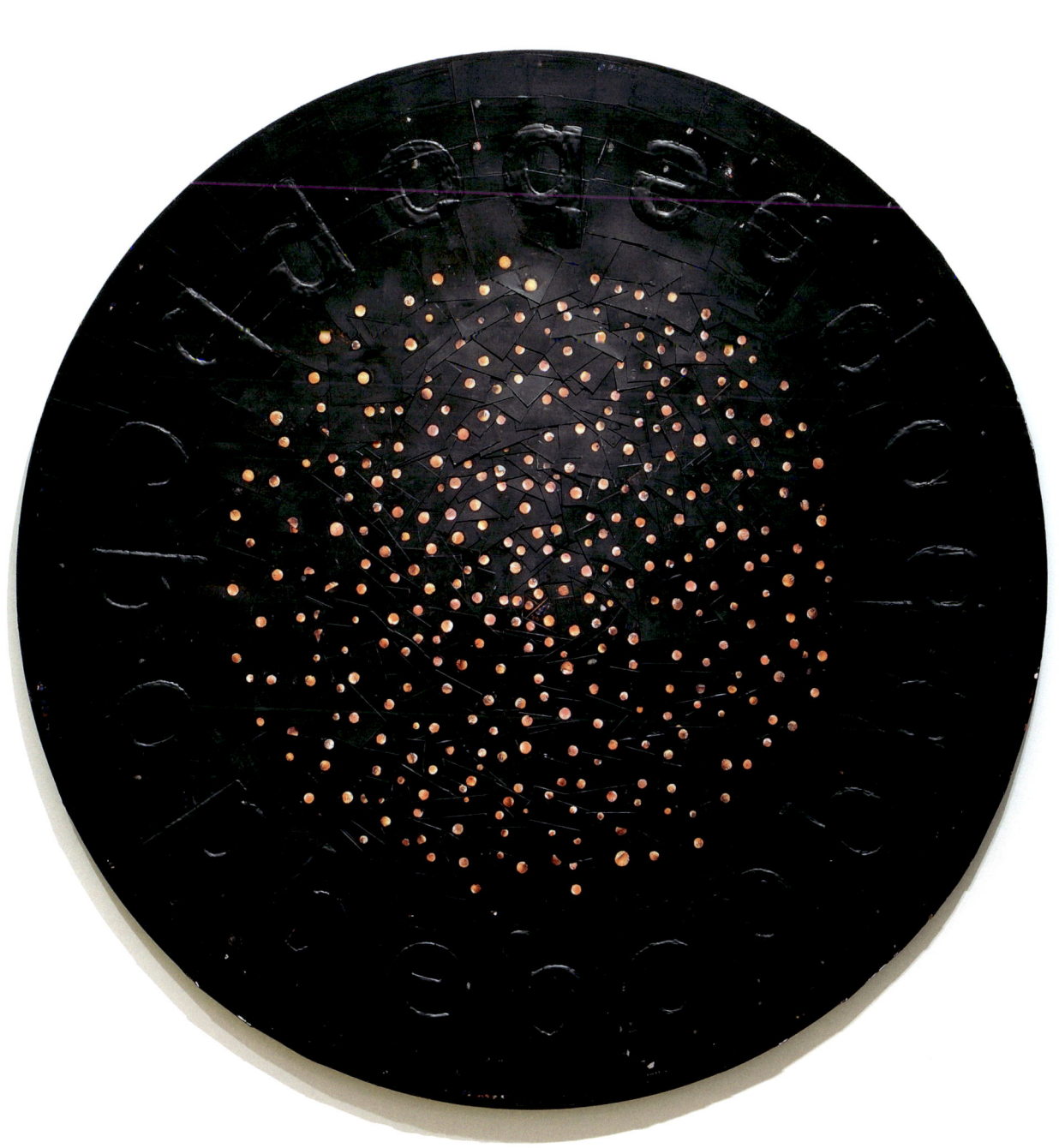

ABOUT THE AUTHORS

Wes Miller has been head men's basketball coach at the University of North Carolina at Greensboro since 2011. Under his leadership, the UNCG Spartans have shared in three regular season Southern Conference championships. In 2018–19, the team won a record twenty-nine games overall. As a student athlete, Miller played in Chapel Hill for the University of North Carolina Tarheels, coached by Roy Williams. In his senior year with that team, he wrote the memoir *The Road to Blue Heaven: An Insider's Diary of North Carolina's 2007 Season*, published by Pegasus Books.

Dr. Emily Stamey has been curator of exhibitions at the Weatherspoon Art Museum since 2015. Prior to joining the Weatherspoon, she served in curatorial posts at the Scottsdale Museum of Contemporary Art in Arizona and the Ulrich Museum of Art at Wichita State University in Kansas. Stamey is the author of *Dread & Delight: Fairy Tales in an Anxious World* (2018) and *Stocked: Contemporary Art from the Grocery Aisles* (2013). A scholar of contemporary art in the United States, she received her BA from Grinnell College in Iowa and her MA and PhD from the University of Kansas—where her studies included sound schooling in Jayhawk basketball.

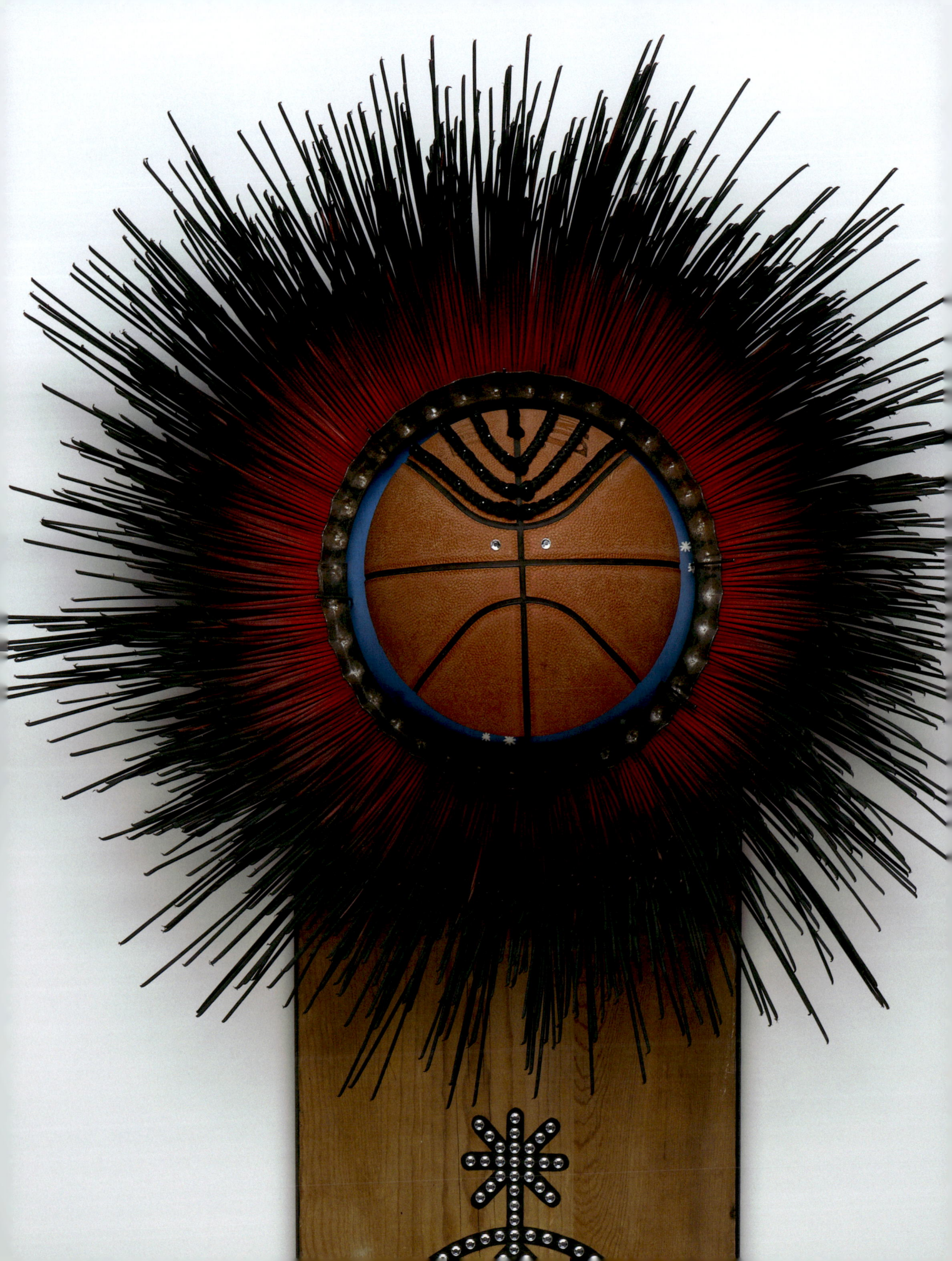

REPRODUCTION CREDITS

Cover © Paul Pfeiffer

p. 6 © Victor Solomon, photo by Geordy Pearson, courtesy of the artist

p. 9 © Suzanne McClelland, photo courtesy of the artist

p. 12 © David Huffman, photo by Jay Jones, courtesy of the artist

p. 14 Bettman Collection via Getty Images

pp. 23–24 © Gina Adams, photos by Aaron Paden, courtesy of the artist and Accola Griefen Fine Art, Brooklyn

p. 27 © Daniel Arsham, photo by Guillaume Ziccarelli, photo courtesy of the artist and Perrotin, New York

pp. 29–31 © Bill Bamberger

p. 33 © Janet Biggs

p. 35 © Mark Bradford, photos courtesy of 21c Museum Hotels, the artist, and Hauser & Wirth

p. 37 © Kendell Carter and Dawn Atlier, photo courtesy of the artists

p. 39 © André Leon Gray, photo courtesy of the artist and the North Carolina Museum of Art, Raleigh

p. 41 © David Hammons, photo courtesy of the Nasher Museum of Art, Durham, North Carolina

p. 43 © David Hilliard, photo courtesy of the artist and Yancey Richardson Gallery, New York

p. 45 © David Huffman, photo by Jay Jones, courtesy of the artist

p. 47 © David Huffman, photo courtesy of the artist

p. 49 © Brian Jungen, photo by Jean Vong, courtesy of the artist

p. 51 © Jeff Koons, photo courtesy of Art Bridges, Bentonville, Arkansas

p. 53 © Suzanne McClelland, photo courtesy of the artist

pp. 55–56 © Esmaa Mohamoud

p. 58 © Maria Molteni and NCAA, photo by Jordan Tynes, courtesy of the artists

p. 59 © Maria Molteni and NCAA, photo courtesy of the artists

pp. 61, 63 © Paul Pfeiffer

p. 65 © Joyce J. Scott, photo by Dhanraj Emanuel, courtesy of the artist and Goya Contemporary Gallery, Baltimore

p. 67 © Lorna Simpson, photo courtesy of the artist and Hauser & Wirth

p. 69 © Victor Solomon, photo by Geordy Pearson, courtesy of the artist

pp. 71–72 © Hank Willis Thomas, photos courtesy of the artist and Jack Shainman Gallery, New York

p. 75 © Nari Ward, photo by Peter Paul Geoffrion, courtesy of the artist; Nasher Museum of Art, Durham, North Carolina; and Lehmann Maupin, New York, Hong Kong, and Seoul

p. 78 © André Leon Gray, photo courtesy of the artist and the North Carolina Museum of Art, Raleigh

André Leon Gray, *Black Magic (It's Fantastic)* (detail), 2005

To the Hoop: Basketball and Contemporary Art is published in conjunction with the exhibition of the same name, organized by the Weatherspoon Art Museum, UNC Greensboro, on view there February 1 through June 7, 2020; and traveling to the Ulrich Museum of Art, Wichita State University, Kansas, August 27 through November 9, 2020.

Library of Congress Control Number: 2019902554
ISBN: 978-1-890949-18-1

Published by Weatherspoon Art Museum
UNC Greensboro
PO Box 26170
Greensboro, North Carolina 27402-6170
www.weatherspoon.uncg.edu

Distributed by the University of North Carolina Press
www.uncpress.org

Produced by Lucia | Marquand, Seattle
www.luciamarquand.com

Edited by Terry Ann R. Neff, t. a. neff associates, inc., Tucson, Arizona
Designed by Meghann Ney
Typeset in Neue Plak by Tina Henderson
Proofread by Bruno George
Color management by iocolor, Seattle
Printed and bound in China by Artron Art Group

Cover: Paul Pfeiffer, *Four Horsemen of the Apocalypse (18)* (detail), 2004

This publication has been generously supported by the Weatherspoon Art Museum's Jane and John Ellison Publications Endowment.

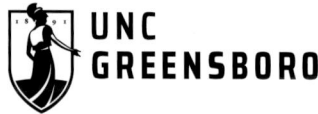

weatherspoon
art museum

UNC
GREENSBORO